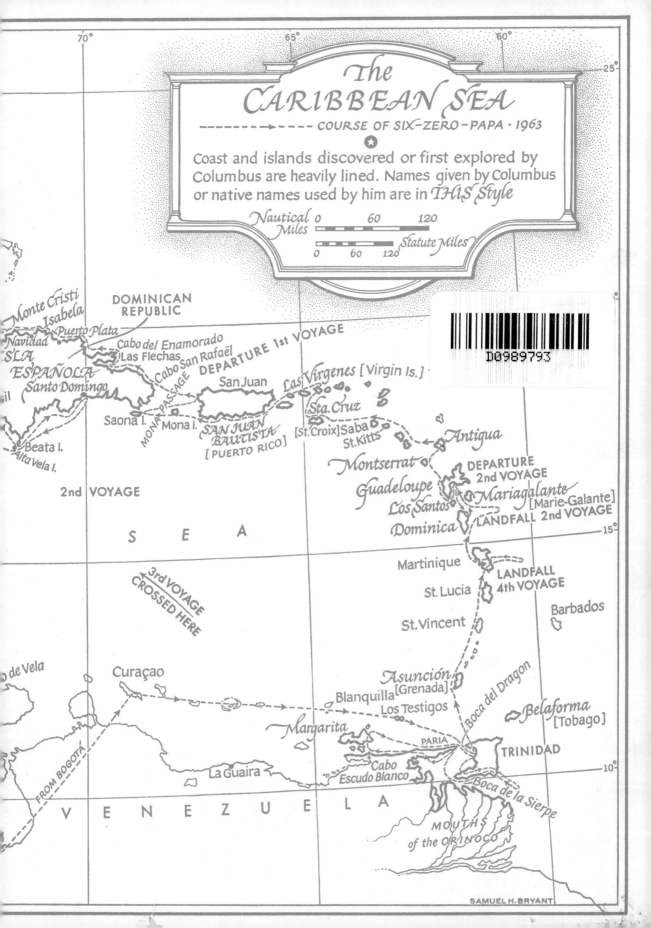

The
CARIBBEAN SEA

------→------ COURSE OF SIX–ZERO–PAPA · 1963
★

Coast and islands discovered or first explored by
Columbus are heavily lined. Names given by Columbus
or native names used by him are in *THIS Style*

Nautical Miles 0   60   120

Statute Miles 0   60   120

DOMINICAN REPUBLIC

Monte Cristi
Isabela
Puerto Plata
Navidad
Cabo del Enamorado
Las Flechas
SLA
ESPAÑOLA
Cabo San Rafaël
DEPARTURE 1st VOYAGE
Santo Domingo
Saona I.
Mona I.
San Juan
Las Virgenes [Virgin Is.]
Sta. Cruz
Beata I.
Alta Vela I.
SAN JUAN BAUTISTA
[PUERTO RICO]
[St.Croix] Saba
St.Kitts
Antigua

2nd VOYAGE

Montserrat
DEPARTURE
2nd VOYAGE
Guadeloupe
Los Santos
Mariagalante
[Marie-Galante]
Dominica
LANDFALL 2nd VOYAGE

S E A

Martinique
LANDFALL
4th VOYAGE
St. Lucia

3rd VOYAGE
CROSSED HERE

St.Vincent
Barbados

de Vela
Curaçao
Asunción
[Grenada]
Blanquilla
Los Testigos
Belaforma
[Tobago]

FROM BOGOTÁ
Margarita
PARIA
TRINIDAD

La Guaira
Cabo Escudo Blanco
Boca del Dragon
Boca de la Sierpe

V E N E Z U E L A
MOUTHS of the ORINOCO

SAMUEL H. BRYANT

The Caribbean
As Columbus Saw It

Waterfall on the Grand Carbet, Guadeloupe
"It was the fairest thing in the world to see from what a height it fell."

The Caribbean
As Columbus Saw It

By
SAMUEL ELIOT MORISON
and
MAURICIO OBREGÓN

Photographs by
David L. Crofoot
Cristina Martinez-Irujo de Obregón
Members of the Harvard Columbus Expedition
and Other Friends

An Atlantic Monthly Press Book

LITTLE, BROWN AND COMPANY · BOSTON · TORONTO

Published simultaneously in Canada
by Little, Brown & Company (Canada) Limited

PRINTED IN THE UNITED STATES OF AMERICA

To the Best of Crews:

Priscilla Barton Morison

Cristina Martinez-Irujo de Obregón

INTRODUCTION

K INGSTON, this is Six-zero-Papa. Over.
Santo Domingo, del Seis-cero-Papá. Cambio.
Pointe-à-Pitre, du Six-zéro-Papa. Terminé.

One or another of these signals was on the air several times daily in the Caribbean during May, June and October 1963. They came from a Cessna-310 airplane carrying Captain Mauricio Obregón, the owner-pilot; Rear Admiral Samuel E. Morison USNR, historian; and David L. Crofoot, photographer, flying a mission to cover every spot in the Caribbean seen by Christopher Columbus.[1] The identification of the plane is HK-960-P; HK standing for Colombia, P for Private Plane, and 960 its number. On the air, by international code, P is understandably pronounced Papa. Usually Six-zero-Papa (or Six-oh-Papa as we sometimes called ourselves) was answered promptly and told to come in to a definite runway. Sometimes there was no answer, which mildly distressed the crew; and once they had to make an emergency unauthorized landing on a grass strip. But everywhere they came through safely and accomplished their mission.

All this started in 1960 when Mark Bortman of Boston, head of the People-to-People program, was asked by Señor Alfonso Mejia of Cartagena, Colombia, to persuade Admiral Morison to visit his country and lecture on Christopher Columbus, tutelar deity of the Republic. The Morisons needed little persuasion. They flew to Colombia in January 1961, delivered lectures at Bogotá and Cartagena, and made friends with several Columbus enthusiasts. One of these, Mauricio Obregón, took Morison on a trial flight to photograph the Sierra Nevada de Santa Marta, and it was then that the idea of this book was born. Why not fly in Obregón's plane all over the Caribbean, photograph every coast and island that Columbus saw, and write a joint book on the subject? That is what we did, after a special photographic window had been installed in the Cessna; and here, reader, is the result.

[1] In the October flight, Señora de Obregón replaced Mr. Crofoot as photographer, and Mrs. Morison came, too.

Int. 1   Obregón already knew this territory from the air; Morison, a seagoing
historian, in the years immediately preceding World War II had covered
this territory under sail — in barkentine *Capitana*, ketch *Mary Otis*, and
sundry native small craft. These voyages, which Captain Paul Hammond
USNR helped Morison to organize, were collectively designated the Harvard
Columbus Expedition. With few exceptions, every place mentioned or seen by
Columbus and his shipmates was identified, and the results appeared in Morison's *Admiral of the Ocean Sea* (1942) and *Christopher Columbus, Mariner*
(1955). In these volumes there was no room for illustrations; and, in any
event, the photographic coverage by members of the Harvard Columbus Expedition was very spotty. Moreover, after examining photographs of the
Caribbean taken from airplanes, Morison concluded that low-level air photographs give one a much better idea of coastal scenery than deck-level snapshots. In these, a superbly picturesque island often appears low and uninter-
esting. One can convey a more accurate idea of how the scenery looked to
Columbus's masthead lookouts as they progressively formed an idea of the
shores they approached by photographing from the air at low altitude. Air
photographs may profitably be supplemented by close-up views taken from
the shore or from small boats, and by pictures of the trees and shrubs mentioned by Columbus. That, too, we have done (Int. 2).

[viii]

The shoreline of the Caribbean has changed surprisingly little since Columbus's day. Excepting Santo Domingo, the principal cities now marked by *hôtels de luxe* and high-rise office buildings were erected at places where Columbus did not touch; and some places which he predicted would be entrepôts of world shipping — Port Saint Nicolas Môle, for example — are more barren of human life than when he saw them. Thus, we were able to skip the tourist and business centers of the West Indies and concentrate on some of the finest unspoiled scenery in the world. The principal changes in the appearance of these shores since Columbus's day were made by the introduction of sugarcane, the banana, and the coconut. We cannot altogether avoid these intrusive plants in our photographs, but ask the reader to remember that several other species of palm, notably the tall royal palm and the thatch palm, are indigenous to the West Indies, and that sugar cane looks not unlike the native reeds that grow near the mouths of rivers; for instance, at the mouth of the Añasco river, Puerto Rico, as shown in our photograph vii.11.

Int.2

Unfortunately, the state of political relations between our respective countries and Cuba did not permit our including that "Pearl of the Antilles" in our itinerary. But Morison had on hand a fairly good coverage of Cuba taken from the *Mary Otis* in 1940, by his Cuban friends, and by the United States Navy and Air Force. For the mainland chapters, IX and X, our photographer was Señora de Obregón; for Chapter I, which was not covered by Six-zero-Papa, the principal photographer was Mrs. Paul Hammond. Almost all the photographs in the other chapters are by David L. Crofoot, a young friend and neighbor of Morison's who became a professional photographer even before leaving college — Harvard 1962. Mauricio Obregón, in addition to being an alumnus of Oxford and of M.I.T., graduated from Harvard in 1943 and is a co-founder of the University of the Andes, Bogotá. Morison, who took his first degree in 1908, had been actively engaged in Columbian studies for more than forty years (Int. 3).

Int.3

The leisurely reconnaissance made from sailing yachts before 1941 enabled us in 1963 to plan each day's flight and to know beforehand exactly what points we should photograph. Readers who are Columbus experts will doubtless find some of our identifications arbitrary. As a result of our airborne observations and the advice of local authorities, two or three identifications made in Morison's books have been revised. We do not think that readers would be interested by these controversies, and have alluded only to those respecting Puerto Rico (Chapter VII) and El Mármol (Chapter X). We merely ask that our choices be respected, if not accepted, as having been made after much research and discussion.

There are disadvantages to seeing the Caribbean by air, while following Columbus. In contrast to traveling by yacht, one has to put up at hotels. At the good ones, situated many miles from the airports, one cannot dine without calypso singers screaming in one's ear, and the only refuge from piped-in music and excessive air conditioning is the bathroom. And whilst paper work is bad enough for yachtsmen, it is far worse for aviators. We had to enter twenty-two sovereign or quasi-sovereign jurisdictions: — the Bahamas, Cuba, Haiti, the Dominican Republic, Puerto Rico, American Virgin Islands, British Virgin Islands, Netherlands West Indies, French Antilles, the rest of the British West Indies, Trinidad-Tobago, Jamaica, Venezuela, Colombia, Panama, the Canal Zone, Mexico, Costa Rica, Guatemala, Nicaragua, Honduras and British Honduras. Each has its own customs service, each requires documents ad infinitum; and some, having recently achieved independence, have staffed their airports with men who do everything by the book and haven't the common sense to modify regulations to meet special circumstances.

All officials in the Caribbean are on the lookout for communist agents or other revolutionaries, and are congenitally suspicious of photographers. Had it not been for Obregón's diplomatic passport as former ambassador to Venezuela and to the O.A.S. in Washington, and for his position as president of the International Aviation Federation, and for the fact that the authorities had been informed beforehand what we were doing, we would never have got through. On more than one occasion when an official cited a regulation wrong, Obregón silenced him by saying, "I was one of the officials who drafted it — I ought to know!" Even so, we spent more time at airports fueling, making minor repairs, arguing, and filling out papers than we did in the air. At one place we were victims of a feud between customs and control tower, which resulted in our having to move Six-zero-Papa thrice across the airfield. Thus, flying through the Caribbean in 1963 was as much of an adventure as motoring across the United States or Spain sixty years earlier; many local people and authorities did not understand it, suspected it, and threw unnecessary difficulties in our way. "Papa Doc" Duvalier's gas drums on Cap Haitien airdrome recalled a barrier with signs forbidding automobiles in 1903, guarded by a bearded sheriff with a shotgun. If the governments in the Caribbean really want visitors by private plane they must simplify their regulations and improve the manners of some of their officials.

Recent changes of regime afforded us many laughs. An official in one island gets a tip by offering to buy American dollars in the local currency; having secured the dollars, he walks away to "make change," never to return. And in another island there was a very ex-British-sergeant-major type — smart uniform, pointed moustache and all — who, when reproved for demanding, late at night, that we fill out a document which he was unable to supply, remarked, "I am here to see that everything is done *properly*," and stalked away with great dignity muttering, "Properly — properly — properly."

Things were very different when we came under Colombian or United States jurisdiction. The United States Air Force gave us permission to use its fields at Ramey, Puerto Rico, and San Salvador; the United States Navy at Guantánamo treated us as honored guests; Colombia admitted the Morisons without a visa.

Briefly relating the story of our flights — which may be followed on the endpaper map — we made our first rendezvous at Port-of-Spain, Trinidad, and spent several days photographing the Columbian sites on that island, the Paria Peninsula, and the islands near Margarita. Under the guidance of Professor J. W. Purseglove of the College of Tropical Agriculture of the University of the West Indies, and with the help of two amiable assistants, Mr. Crofoot photographed specimens of trees and plants which Columbus and his shipmates had observed; their often puzzling descriptions having been previously identified by botanists of Cuba, of Harvard University, and by Professor Purseglove himself. On one occasion, weather forced us to make an emergency landing on a strip at Point Fortin maintained by Shell Oil. From Port-of-Spain we took off for the Lesser Antilles on an overcast day when photography was difficult; but Crofoot took some good ones of the little bay of Sainte-Luce, Martinique, where Columbus's men went ashore and washed in the river after their landfall on the Fourth Voyage. At Guadeloupe, thanks to the overcast, which must have been of the same depth as the one that greeted Columbus, Crofoot obtained remarkable photographs of the waterfall that seems to come from the clouds (see frontispiece and Chapter VI). We also photographed the various coves where Columbus anchored, the island Marie-Galante that he named after his ship, and Les Saintes, which he named after All Saints' Day.

While the Morisons luxuriated in the bathing at La Caravelle, St. Ann's, and drove about Guadeloupe, Obregón and Crofoot — thanks to the former's friend at Pointe-à-Pitre, the Comte de Gennes — made a brief excursion to Dominica, which many consider the loveliest island in the West Indies. Their objective was the Carib reservation, which they attained on foot after abandoning their jeep — our photograph of the road (vi.7) will show why — and losing Crofoot's passport in the mud. With the aid of the Caribs' priest and protector Father Martin, they found and photographed some of the last of that race which fought so valiantly against Spaniards, French and English, and which now numbers only a few hundred souls.

Next day was devoted to the Lesser Antilles — Montserrat, Antigua, Nevis, St. Kitts, St. Eustatius, and Saba, ending at St. Croix, where Mrs. Morison was waiting. Crofoot covered the harbor there now called Salt River Bay, where Columbus had his first fight with Indians. Thence we flew to Virgin Gorda at the east end of the archipelago which Columbus named after St. Ursula and her eleven thousand seagoing virgin martyrs. We threaded the entire group, debouched by the Francis Drake Channel into the bay between St. Thomas and St. John, covered Vieques, ranged the southern coast of Puerto Rico, rounded Cape Rojo at the southwestern end; and after a brief trip across the Mona Channel to photograph Cape Engaño and Saona and Mona islands, landed at Ramey Field, Puerto Rico. There we learned from a customs official that the Virgins were a foreign country so far as Puerto Rico was concerned; but, having bought nothing in St. Croix but a pair of socks, we had no duty to pay. And the United States Air Force gave us V.I.P. hospitality, bless them!

This photographic flying, with frequent swoops from high to low altitude to photograph places noticed by Columbus and his shipmates, was exhausting to all hands. We always carried a sandwich-and-coffee lunch, but were mighty glad of a bath, a good dinner and a soft bed at the end of each day's run. And Crofoot, whose youthful energy never damped down, often stayed up late at night developing his films.

Now occurred our first political complication. "Papa Doc" Duvalier, president of Haiti, was giving himself a second term and throwing into jail everyone who objected, and the Dominican Republic was threatening to invade his country. Consequently, all foreigners were ordered to stay away from Haiti, where, moreover, the airfields had been blocked with gasoline drums. So we had to cut out a scheduled call at Cap Haitien, and to photograph the Haitian coast from a safe distance, out of reach of possible antiaircraft fire. When Morison asked his partner why the Haitians had not badgered us over the radio, Obregón replied that he had used a frequency special for such occasions — *off!* This did not prevent us from obtaining some excellent shots of both the north and south coasts of Hispaniola; and these we have spliced out with photographs taken from boats and ashore in 1939.

We made a fueling call at Great Inagua Island, where the salt ponds and coral shoals make the most superb color contrasts to be found in the West Indies. The weather then closed in, and we had to perform a tricky bit of navigation to find the small but important Cay St. Domingo. A thunderstorm forced Six-zero-Papa off course; but we made a 90-degree turn at the right time, sighted the diminutive cay through a gap in the clouds, and swooped down to photograph it. The weather then cleared opportunely for us to photograph Crooked Island, Long Island, and Rum Cay, and to make a good reconnaissance of San Salvador. There, although arriving two days earlier than expected, we were most hospitably received and entertained by Mrs. Ruth Wolper, the Lady Bountiful of the island, at her beautiful estate Polaris, where she has established the New World Museum of local Indian artifacts and Columbian relics. By car we visited the site of Columbus's first landing, now marked by a cross; and by a motorboat piloted by a United States Naval Facility officer we cruised through Graham's Harbor and around the island.

Next, we flew south through the Bahamas, rounded Cape Maisí, Cuba, and landed at the United States Naval Base, Guantánamo, dodging howitzer practice during the final approach. There we were royally entertained by Admiral James W. Davis USN and taken around the perimeter, which has become a miniature Berlin wall, heavily guarded but still surmountable by freedom-seeking defectors. From Guantánamo we flew over Navassa Island, which saved the lives of Méndez and Fieschi in their canoe crossing of 1503, photographed the southern coasts of Haiti and the Dominican Republic, and came down at Punta Caucedo, the airport of Santo Domingo.

The Dominicans were celebrating the second anniversary of their "third liberation" — the first having been from Spain, the second from Haiti, and the third from Trujillo. Grounded by weather, we spent two pleasant days examining the antiquities of Santo Domingo, which Bartholomew Columbus founded in 1495 — the oldest city in the New World which has enjoyed a continuous existence.

Our flight from Santo Domingo westward was uneventful until we approached the island where Columbus, unwillingly, spent an entire year. An electrical storm had built up over Jamaica, everything ahead was thick as pea soup, and frequent transmissions of *Kingston — This is Six-zero-Papa — Over* brought no reply. When Obregón was about ready to turn back and seek the forbidden hospitality of Haiti, deliverance appeared in the shape of a grass field at Pera near Morant Point, the eastern end of Jamaica, where we negotiated an emergency landing on the bumpy surface. Once down, thankful to be alive, and drenched by torrential rain, we were approached by the stern guardian of the field with an order to clear out! (See photographs xi. 11, 12.) That, of course, we declined to do; and the guardian, relenting, allowed us to secure the Cessna for the night, and procured a car and driver to take us, very wet and exhausted, to Kingston. It turned out that the field was owned by Mr. Johnson of Kingston, who sprays the banana plantations and cane fields from the air; and he, as soon as we telephoned our plight to him, was kindness itself.

While Morison proceeded by car, with the baggage, to join Mrs. Morison at Montego Bay, Obregón and Crofoot painfully, through overcast and rain, flew from the grass strip to Kingston, then to a small airstrip on the north coast, and thence to Montego Bay. Here we had a real rest, for Montego Bay is charming out of season, as this was.

The weather now closed in so thick to the westward, and reports of it on the Honduran coast were so unfavorable, that on 5 June, after one attempt to reach the Caymans and being forced back by a wall of cumulonimbus clouds, we decided to postpone the mainland leg of our journey until October. Crofoot returned to New York; the Morisons flew with Obregón to Bogotá, where they enjoyed days of Colombian hospitality before flying back to Boston.

On the mainland leg in October, the participants were both Obregóns and both Morisons, Señora de Obregón taking the photographs and Mrs. Morison acting as honorary co-pilot. These ladies had already become friends in Bogotá, and their association on this flight brought them very closely together. Incidentally, they discovered that they were cousins. Thomas McKean, signer of the Declaration of Independence and Governor of Pennsylvania, had two daughters: Sally, who married the Marqués del Casa Yrujo, first Spanish minister to the United States; and Letitia, who married Dr. George Buchanan of Philadelphia. Señora de Obregón is descended from the one, and Mrs. Morison from the other.

On 20 October 1963 the Morisons joined the Obregóns at Acapulco, Mexico, to begin their flight in Six-zero-Papa along the mainland. We flew over the Sierra Madre and a part of Guatemala (where we were warned not to stop — that republic being under a "state of siege") to Belize, British Honduras. This little colonial capital has been almost completely rebuilt since the destructive hurricane of 1961, and has a simple but excellent hotel provided with a swimming pool, but free of musical nuisances. We were much amused by the customs official of whom we inquired what was going on in Guatemala. With all the dignity of a crown official (portraits of Queen Elizabeth and Prince Philip in his office), he replied, "Oh, just the usual thing in these republics, sir!"

By 11 A.M. next day we were over the Bay Islands of Honduras, and Señora de Obregón unlimbered her Leica to take the striking photograph of Guanaja (Bonacca) with which our Chapter IX opens. From there we made Cape Honduras and flew eastward along the Honduran coast, looking for Columbus's Río de la Posesión, which we identified as the Río Romano. Thence along the coast, around Cape Gracias a Dios and to Puerto Limón, Costa Rica, making emergency calls at Puerto Cabezas and Bluefields, Nicaragua, for fueling and small repairs. At Bluefields we encountered a young American "duster" pilot, one of those employed to spray insecticide on banana plantations. Ten days earlier, another "duster," Mr. Anderson, had crashed in the Nicaraguan jungle and our acquaintance had spent every day in the air searching in vain for some trace of him. Eventually, Anderson found his way to the coast on foot, and was rescued.

Another day took us into the Almirante and Chiriquí Lagoons of the Republic of Panama, along the coast of Veragua, across the Isthmus and to Panama City, where we lay over a day on account of bad weather. The gods did not favor us with fairer weather than Columbus experienced on that "Coast of Contrarieties," as he called it; the rain and overcast along the Panama coast were really menacing to a small plane.

Next, we recrossed the Isthmus of Panama, photographed the spot near the canal entrance where Columbus kept Christmas 1502, passed Puerto Bello and Nombre de Dios, and then flew along the Archipelago de las Mulatas, searching for the point which Columbus named El Mármol, whence he and his two leaky caravels took off for Jamaica on 1 May 1503. It had formerly been identified as Punta de Mosquitos, Panama; but we have upset that (see Chapter X) by identifying it as Cabo Tiburón, Colombia, which has strata and patches of white stone that suggested marble to Columbus. Thence we flew to Bogotá, where our expedition disbanded after a very happy week of flying.

This book is not arranged in the order of our flight, or of Columbus's voyages, but by geography. It seemed to us that that order would be easiest for the reader, rather than frequently returning him to the same place by describing Columbus's four voyages. Chapter I relates, briefly, the approach to the New World from Gomera in the Canaries. San Salvador, the first landfall, comes next, and is followed by the rest of the Bahamas where Columbus touched. Then Cuba, both the north coast of Oriente Province covered in his First Voyage, and the south coast of the Second Voyage. Hispaniola (Haiti and the Dominican Republic), the coast of which was gradually unfolded to Columbus on all four voyages, follows Cuba. We now reverse course and, starting from Martinique, cover the Lesser Antilles, the Virgin Islands and Puerto Rico from southeast to northwest, because Columbus discovered them that way and his descriptions fit that approach. Cutting back to Trinidad, we depict the Third Voyage landfall on that island, the Bocas, and both sides of the Paria Peninsula of Venezuela up to Margarita. The mainland part of the Fourth Voyage, from the Bay Islands, Honduras, to the Gulf of Darien, is covered by Chapters IX and X and is followed by Jamaica, where Columbus spent an unhappy year marooned, at the end of his last voyage.

Here is a summary of the four famous voyages, together with the chapters where our observations on them may be found:—

I Voyage, 1492-93. Bahamas, northeast Cuba, north coast of Hispaniola. Chapters I, II, III, IV, V.

II Voyage, 1493-96. Leeward Islands, Virgin Islands, Puerto Rico, Hispaniola, south coast of Cuba, Jamaica. Chapters IV, V, VI, VII, and XI.

III Voyage, 1498. Trinidad, Gulf of Paria, Margarita, southern Hispaniola. Chapters V and VIII.

IV Voyage, 1502-04. Windward Islands, Hispaniola, mainland from Honduras to Gulf of Darien, and Jamaica. Chapters V, VI, IX, X and XI.

A comparison of Columbus's means and methods of navigation by sea with ours by air is significant, both of scientific progress and of the navigator's continual dependence on certain essentials. The principal difference is in speed. The maximum that Columbus's ships made was 5 knots on the wind, close-hauled, or 11 knots with wind on the quarter or running free. Six-zero-Papa has a cruising speed of 180 knots (nautical miles per hour), increased or decreased by wind. Under conditions such as a flat calm, head wind or contrary set of current, a caravel made no progress whatsoever; whilst a plane such as ours can always wait, grounded, for fair weather or, in most parts of the world today, land if foul weather is threatened, or proceed "on instruments" if not engaged in photography. Columbus required 28 days to cover the Honduran coast from the mouth of his Río de la Posesión to Cape Gracias a Dios, beating against wind and current and anchoring every night. It took us a little more than an hour, including many changes of course to take photographs.

As for methods, both Columbus and we relied on dead reckoning, as it is called in English, with the three basic elements — direction, speed and time. Columbus got his direction from a mariner's magnetic compass much like ours; his card was graduated into 32 points, ours into 360 degrees; variation he could figure by ascertaining true north from a shadow of the sun at noon.

Six-zero-Papa for direction has only an improvement of the same basic nature — a magnetic compass on which the gyrocompass is set. We also have a radio compass which points at any shore station emitting radio waves, thus giving us its direction from the plane; but this is often unreliable when most needed, in an electric storm. Speed through the water Columbus could calculate only by his experienced eye, for no log to measure speed had yet been invented. We have an indicator which gives speed in knots, relative to the ambient air; but we have to apply "by guess and by God" a factor for wind speed and direction, as Columbus did for ocean currents and leeway.

The third factor, time, Columbus obtained from an *ampolleta*, a sand glass which had to be inverted every half hour when the sand ran out; mistakes could be corrected when the sun reached its maximum altitude at noon. We of course had an electric clock set for Greenwich time, as well as our own watches set for local time, when we managed to figure it. Celestial navigation was little used by Columbus, and when he tried it from shipboard his results were wildly inaccurate, but he ascertained the latitude of St. Ann's Bay, Jamaica, fairly accurately by using a primitive quadrant or astrolabe from his grounded ships to obtain the altitude of the North Star. (A mariner's astrolabe of the same model that Columbus used is depicted in our illustration viii. 12.) We did not need to use celestial navigation in the Caribbean, although if we had to fly the Atlantic we would use a bubble octant to establish our position from the heavenly bodies. Thus, both Columbus and we, as a last resort, had to fall back on dead reckoning — compass direction, estimated speed, and time. Both he and we had to make quick decisions: Columbus in darkness or thick weather when he heard breakers or when a squall approached his ships; we when airfields were "socked in" by weather.

We felt that our most important gadget which Columbus lacked was radio telephone, enabling us to communicate with the land, and to receive advance notice of bad weather. Not that radio would have done Columbus much good. Imagine his approaching San Salvador, calling, *"Cipangu, Cipangu: del Santa María, capitana de la flota Castellana. Cambio."* Or, putting Luis de Torres at the mike to talk Arabic to the Grand Khan at Holguin! But we envy the simplicity of Columbus's method of transport. He never had to fill out a manifest or file a sailing plan; imagine the port official at Gomera saying, "I won't accept this 'west to the Indies' destination — everyone knows the Indies lie south and east!" He had no currency problems, and cacao beans were the only native money he encountered; no customs official asked him to declare hawk's bells and glass beads, or to pay harbor dues. But Columbus, like us, had a fueling problem; he had to keep up the supply of firewood, or subsist on cold victuals.

Now a few words as to the sources, all quotations from which are Morison's translation. Columbus's *Diario* or Journal of the First Voyage, as abstracted by Las Casas, and his Letter to the Sovereigns are the principal authorities for the initial voyage of discovery. For the Second Voyage we have the Letter of the fleet surgeon Dr. Diego Alvarez Chanca, the letters of Michele de Cuneo, Nicolo Syllacio's tract based on letters of Guillermo Coma, and Andrés Bernáldez *Historia de los Reyes Católicos*. For the Third Voyage, Las Casas's abstract of Columbus's Journal still exists, and two long letters by the Admiral himself. For the Fourth and last voyage we have the biography of the Admiral by his son who sailed with him, Ferdinand Columbus's *Historie;* Columbus's *Lettera Rarissima* to the Sovereigns, and the narrative of Diego Méndez. Translations of all these sources, except of Chanca and Bernáldez, will be found in Morison's *Journals and Other Documents on the Life and Voyages of Christopher Columbus*, published by the Limited Editions Club, New York, 1964. Text and translation of Dr. Chanca and Andrés Bernáldez are in Cecil Jane *Select Documents Illustrating the Four Voyages of Columbus* (Hakluyt Society, 1930). Other early authorities occasionally quoted in our text are Bartolomé de las Casas *Historia de las Indías*, written between 1550 and 1563, of which the best edition is Lewis Hanke's (3 vols., Mexico D.F., 1951); Peter Martyr *De Orbe Novo* (1516), of which there are many translations, and Gonzalo Fernández de Oviedo *Historia General y Natural de las Indias* (1535), from which we have reproduced several illustrations.

Many people have helped us to complete our flying mission, and this book. President Kennedy of the United States and President Valencia of Colombia furthered our enterprise by requesting their respective foreign and military services to look after us, which they very well did. From the John Simon Guggenheim Memorial Foundation we received a grant toward our expenses. Mrs. Ruth G. Wolper, in addition to her hospitality at Polaris, filled gaps in our photography from her own collection, as did the National Geographic Society, the Navy and the Air Force, from theirs. At Ramey Field, Puerto Rico, we were the guests of the United States Air Force, and at Guantánamo, Cuba, of the United States Navy. At Santo Domingo, Lieutenant Colonel Bevon T. Cass USMC helped us to get about.

Several men of science have helped us to identify the flora mentioned by Columbus and his shipmates: notably Professor J. W. Purseglove of the University of the West Indies, St. Augustine, Trinidad; Brother Alain Liogier, now an exile from his native Cuba; the late Brother León of Colegio La Salle, Havana; and Professors Paul C. Mangelsdorf, Reed C. Rollins and Duncan Clement of Harvard University. For information on the Spanish Main we are indebted to the Honorable Aaron Brown, American ambassador to Nicaragua, and to Don Eduardo Pérez Valle, the leading historian of that Republic; and for information on the Indians of that region, to Dr. Victor W. von Hagen and Dr. Samuel K. Lothrop. Dr. Aurelio Tió of San Juan helped us to determine Columbus's landing place in Puerto Rico.

Finally, we owe a particular debt to those who inspected and made minor repairs to Six-zero-Papa at Bogotá, Ramey, St. Croix and Guantánamo; for without their efficient work we might not have survived to write the book.

SAMUEL E. MORISON
MAURICIO OBREGÓN

Contents

List of Illustrations

Photographs are by David L. Crofoot unless otherwise indicated. The following abbreviations are used:

C.M.-I.deO.   By Señora de Obregón
H.C.E.   By members of the Harvard Columbus Expedition
U.S.N.   By United States Navy
U.S.A.F.   By United States Air Force
A.A.A.F.   By American Army Air Force

Frontispiece

Waterfall on the Grand Carbet, Guadeloupe
"It was the fairest thing in the world to see from what a height it fell."

Chapter III: On to Cathay

Chapter IV: Cuba

Chapter XI: Jamaica

The Caribbean
As Columbus Saw It

i.1

CHAPTER I

West to the Indies

COLUMBUS'S approach to his great discovery required years of thought, planning, persuasion and preparation. These we shall pass over; but we must briefly remind the reader of his transatlantic crossing, the first in history, which brought him to the Caribbean.

His fleet consisted of the *nao* or ship *Santa María*, Juan de la Cosa master and owner, about 85 feet long, with a crew of 40 officers and men; caravel *Pinta*, about 75 feet long, Martín Alonso Pinzón captain, with 25 officers and men; and caravel *Niña*, about 70 feet long, Vicente Yañez Pinzón captain, with 22 officers and men.[1] They were fine, staunch vessels, "well suited for such an enterprise," as Columbus himself wrote. Several attempts have been made in recent years to build "replicas" of these vessels, but there can be no real replica where there are neither plans nor pictures of the originals. The *Santa María III* (i.1) built in 1927, designed by Capitán de Navío Julio Guillén Tato, the leading naval archaeologist of Europe, is as near the original as we are likely ever to get, and she has been copied for the New York World's Fair of 1964. Our photograph shows her under way in a light wind, aided by two long sweeps, standard equipment in 1492. Our second photograph (i.2), of a *Santa María* built at Barbados in 1948 for the J. Arthur Rank film *Christopher Columbus*, is more lively, but the hang of the sails suggests that her motive power at the moment was a concealed gasoline engine.

Columbus's gateway to the Caribbean, his point of departure for the New World on three of his four voyages, was San Sebastián, Island of Gomera, in

---

[1] Every Spanish vessel at this period had an official name, usually that of a saint who was supposed to look after her, and a nickname based on that of her owner, place of origin, or sailing qualities. *Santa María's* nickname *La Gallega* (The Galician) was seldom used. We do not know the official name of *Pinta*. That of *Niña* was *Santa Clara;* she was nicknamed after the Niño family, who owned her.

i.2

the Canaries. In the roadstead there the two caravels joined his flagship on 2 September 1492. San Sebastián, as shown from the deck of our *Capitana* in 1939 (i.3), is very little changed from the newly founded Spanish colonial town of Columbus's day. The church where he worshipped, and the stone Torre del Conde, part of the castle where he was entertained, are still there. His hostess was the young, beautiful and energetic Doña Beatriz de Peraza y Bobadilla, widow of the captain who had conquered Gomera, then acting captain while waiting for a new one to be appointed. We have it on the authority of Columbus's shipmate Michele de Cuneo that the Admiral became *tincto d'amore* with this lady — fell head over heels in love with her; and she gave him a splendid reception when he returned to begin his Second Voyage. Beyond that, we know naught of this romance. It may be surmised that Doña

Beatriz did not want a sailor for a second husband, but a fighting man who would settle down and protect her and her infant son, the first Conde de Gomera. It was her cousin, Francisco de Bobadilla, who sent Columbus home in chains after his Third Voyage.

At San Sebastián, Columbus, like the provident shipmaster that he was, filled with water numerous barrels which the coopers put together from oak staves, loaded firewood for the galley, and bought casks of salt beef and cheeses, a Gomera specialty. There was no shortage of food, fuel or water on this pioneering voyage.

In the Church of the Assumption, where the Admiral and his officers and men heard their last mass before sailing on 6 September 1492, the present priest, Father Velásquez, held a special service for our Harvard Columbus Expedition four centuries and a half later. Our photograph (i.4) shows the head of the local *falange*, James McGregor Byrne (now an ambassador in the foreign service), Father Velásquez, John W. McElroy (now Rear Admiral USNR), and the Governor of Gomera holding our American yacht ensign and the banner of the Harvard Columbus Expedition. In the service that followed, the Padre blessed our ship and ourselves, and thanked God that someone at last was seeking *veritas* about the great Discoverer. Our *Capitana* had the honor of an enthusiastic send-off from almost the entire male population of San Sebastián, when we weighed anchor for our ocean crossing.

Columbus's First Voyage to the New World, the most momentous ocean passage in modern history, was also one of the easiest in terms of wind and

[5]

i.4

weather. For this, the Admiral's maritime experience and natural sagacity were largely responsible. The Azores as a jumping-off place would have put him several hundred miles farther west, but he wished to avoid bucking the westerly winds which had thwarted Portuguese mariners seeking land beyond Corvo and Flores. So he dropped down to the Canaries, which he knew to be within the belt of easterly tradewinds, and chose, for point of departure, the westernmost Canary Island which Spain had subdued. Thus he cut some 600 miles off the ocean passage and, what was more important, could count on a fair wind for at least part of the voyage; actually, the fleet scudded before the wind most of the way. And the season that he chose was free of hurricanes, though not of storms. Call it luck, divine favor, or what you will; had Columbus deliberately set out to discover a New World instead of (as he intended) a sea route to the Indies, he could not have chosen stouter ships, a better route, or a more propitious time of year for his adventure.

For two days after leaving Gomera the fleet lay becalmed, but at 3 A.M. 8 September "the northeast wind began to blow, and he shaped his course to the west." Next day they passed Hierro (Ferro), outermost of the Canary group. The next ten days of the voyage were pure joy. "The Admiral here says," abstracts Las Casas for September 16, "*que era placer grande el gusto de las mañanas"* — that the savor of the mornings was a great delight. What memories that phrase evokes to modern seafarers! A fragrant, cool freshness of daybreak in the trades, the false dawn shooting up a pyramid of grayish-white light, the paling stars and the navigators bustling about to shoot their favorites in the brief morning twilight of the tropics, rosy lights on the clouds as sunrise approaches, sudden transformation of the squaresails from dark gray to ruddy gold, smell of dew drying from the deck, the general feeling of God's in his heaven and all's right with the world (i.5). "The weather was like April in Andalusia," logged Columbus, and "the only thing wanting was to hear the nightingale."

i.5

There was no lack of other birds — Wilson's petrels, boobies, Arctic terns, the forked-tail *rabiforcado* or man o'war bird, the tropic bird (*rabo de junco* — "reed-tail," Columbus called it); old-time seamen call it the boatswain bird because its tail suggests a marlinspike. Two flew on board our *Capitana* in mid-ocean (i.6). Columbus and his men, no ornithologists, thought that their appearance indicated land. Another bird noted by Columbus alighting on his flagship to rest he called *tórtola*, the mourning dove; and a mourning dove flew on board our *Capitana* too. Here he is (i.7), caught like the tropic bird by Susy Hammond's camera, refuting by his visit the ornithologist who told us Columbus must have been mistaken, that no dove could fly that far out to sea! And many *peces golondrinas*, flying fish, flew on board and were eagerly cooked and eaten.

i.6

i

Columbus's crews were not, as sometimes represented, a lot of jailbirds; they were mostly seamen and boys from the Huelva region of Spain, recruited by the two captains Pinzón. But like all sailors of every age prior to ours, they were conservative in the sense of being superstitious, and suspicious of anything outside their experience. The first evidence of their uneasiness appeared when they entered the Sargasso Sea and the ocean seemed to be one vast meadow of green and yellow gulfweed (i.8), in which they feared to be stuck,

especially since the wind became light and variable. But gulfweed is no hindrance to navigation, as Columbus already knew; and he even tried a cast of lead to satisfy his men that they were not running onto rocks. The 200-fathom lead line found no bottom; no wonder, as the ocean is some 2300 fathoms deep at that point.

The next excitement was a false landfall. As may be seen from the drawing taken from Martin Behaim's globe of 1492, which follows very closely the sailing directions suggested to Columbus years earlier by Paolo Toscanelli of Florence (i.9), the latitude of the Canaries, which eventually would cut Cipangu (Japan), passes very close to an island called Antilia or Cete Cidades (Seven Cities). Antilia — the name means simply "Island Over Against" Portugal — was supposed to have been settled by seven groups of Portuguese refugees from the wars with the Moors, in the eighth century. Every mapmaker of the Middle Ages placed Antilia, as well as the mythical isles of St. Brandan and Brazil (which Behaim also marked), somewhere in the Atlantic beyond the Azores. Columbus hoped to locate Antilia as a convenient staging point for future voyages to the Indies. On 25 September, when land was

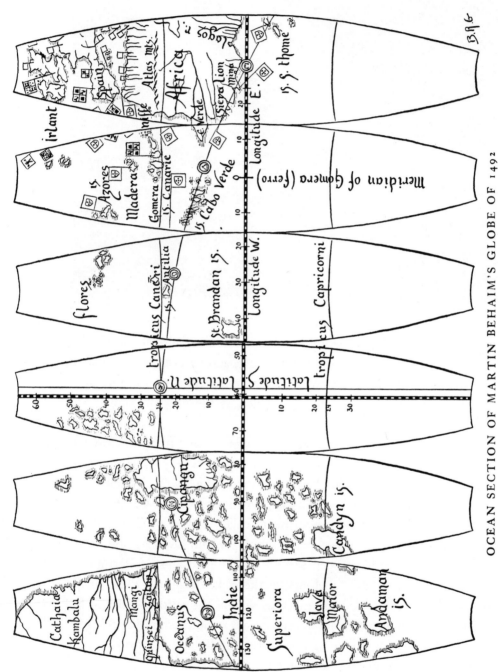

OCEAN SECTION OF MARTIN BEHAIM'S GLOBE OF 1492

Equator and Latitude Meridian as in Original. Degree Numbers Added.

i.9

reported at sunset, he concluded, "This is it!" The Admiral ordered *Gloria in Excelsis Deo* to be sung and altered course to suit; but in the morning no land was there. Only a cloud on the horizon.

Columbus was not greatly disturbed by this false landfall, since his main object was to sail to the Indies, and he had already made about two thirds of the calculated distance. His Journal reflects only serenity, and joy at the beauty of the ocean. "The sea was like a river, the air sweet and very soft . . . the air was very sweet and savory . . . the sea flat as a river" (i.10). Another week of fair wind and calm sea followed — "Thanks to God," recorded the Admiral. The reason he found the ocean so smooth was that he was skirting the northerly edge of the easterly tradewinds, which had had no chance to build up a big sea.

i.10

More birds now appeared; and they were responsible for one of the most vital decisions made on this First Voyage. On Sunday, 7 October 1492, observing flocks of them passing over the ships in a southwesterly direction, the Admiral, remembering that the Portuguese had discovered islands by following the flight of birds, decided to alter course from west to west-southwest. He had actually encountered the autumn migration from northern America to the West Indies. Next day was one of light airs, "soft as in April in Seville, and it is a pleasure to be in it, so fragrant it is." There speaks the seaman and the artist. The ocean, whether calm or disturbed, emits a delicious odor which some old salts prefer to that of the warm earth, flowers and other growing things; Columbus loved them both. More land birds now appeared, and "all night they heard birds passing."

On Wednesday the 10th, when a brisk easterly breeze returned and the caravels made best speed westward, mutiny flared on board. "The people could stand it no longer and complained of the long voyage; but the Admiral cheered them as best he could, holding out good hope of the advantages they would have. And he added that it was useless to complain, *he had come to go to the Indies*, and so had to continue until he found them, with the aid of Our Lord." *Pinta* and *Niña* approached the flagship by signal. Columbus conferred with the Pinzóns by shouting as the two handy caravels shot under the *Santa María*'s high poop, and the Admiral was supported by Martín Alonso Pinzón of *Pinta* crying out, "*Adelante! Adelante!*"— Sail on! Sail on! But the Admiral had to promise his men to turn back if they failed to sight land within three days.

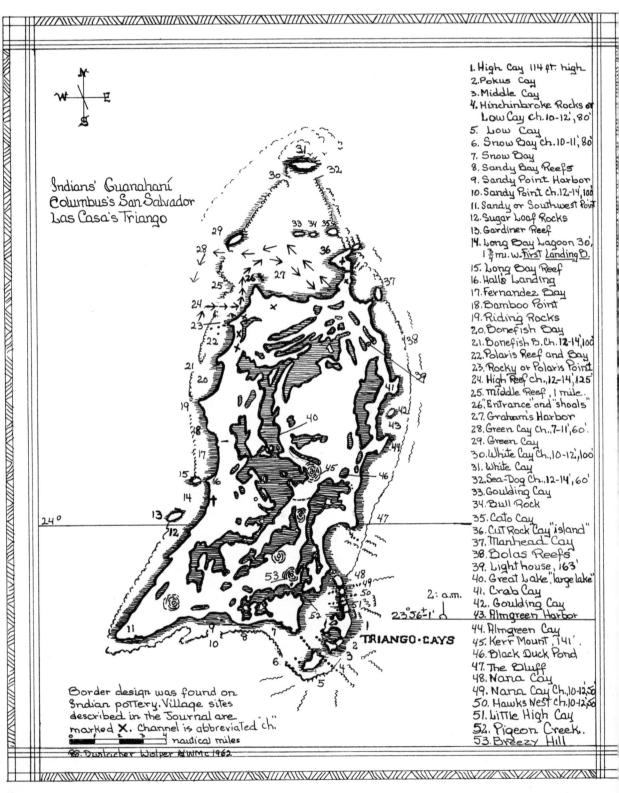

Indians' Guanahaní
Columbus's San Salvador
Las Casa's Triango

1. High Cay 114 ft. high
2. Pokus Cay
3. Middle Cay
4. Hinchinbroke Rocks or Low Cay Ch. 10-12', 80'
5. Low Cay
6. Snow Bay Ch. 10-11', 80'
7. Snow Bay
8. Sandy Bay Reefs
9. Sandy Point Harbor
10. Sandy Point Ch. 12-14', 100'
11. Sandy or Southwest Point
12. Sugar Loaf Rocks
13. Gardiner Reef
14. Long Bay Lagoon 30', 1 3/4 mi. w. First Landing D.
15. Long Bay Reef
16. Hall's Landing
17. Fernandez Bay
18. Bamboo Point
19. Riding Rocks
20. Bonefish Bay
21. Bonefish B. Ch. 12-14', 100'
22. Polaris Reef and Bay
23. Rocky or Polaris Point
24. High Reef Ch. 12-14', 125'
25. Middle Reef, 1 mile
26. "Entrance" and "shoals"
27. Graham's Harbor
28. Green Cay Ch. 7-11', 60'
29. Green Cay
30. White Cay Ch. 10-12', 100'
31. White Cay
32. Sea-Dog Ch. 12-14', 60'
33. Goulding Cay
34. Bull Rock
35. Cato Cay
36. Cut Rock Cay "island"
37. Manhead Cay
38. Dolas Reefs
39. Lighthouse, 163'
40. Great Lake "large lake"
41. Crab Cay
42. Goulding Cay
43. Almgreen Harbor
44. Almgreen Cay
45. Kerr Mount, 141'
46. Black Duck Pond
47. The Bluff
48. Nana Cay
49. Nana Cay Ch. 10-12', 50'
50. Hawks Nest ch. 10-12', 80'
51. Little High Cay
52. Pigeon Creek
53. Breezy Hill

2: a.m.
23°56±1'
TRIANGO·CAYS

24°

Border design was found on Indian pottery. Village sites described in the Journal are marked X. Channel is abbreviated "ch."

0 1 2 3 4 nautical miles

P.S. Dunlacher Wolper AtWMc 1962

ii. 1

CHAPTER II

San Salvador

ON THURSDAY, 11 October, sailing rapidly to the west-southwest in a heavy sea, the sailors began to see signs of land, such as a floating green branch with wild roses; and "with these signs everyone breathed more freely and grew cheerful." At about ten o'clock that evening Columbus himself saw what he took to be a light, "like a little wax candle lifting and rising, which . . . the Admiral was certain to be near land." He summoned all hands to sing the *Salve Regina*, urged lookouts to keep a sharp watch, and promised a silk doublet to him who should first sight land.

What was this disappearing light, seen when the fleet was still twenty to thirty miles from land? Many and fantastic have been the explanations: — Indians torching for fish (on that rough night!); a luminous jellyfish; sea-worms engaged in courtship; the Light of the World flashing a signal to Christopher; or a mere ocular delusion common among sailors when eagerly searching for land through fog or darkness. Mrs. Ruth Wolper of San Salvador has made the first rational explanation. Observing that the Negroes who now inhabit San Salvador light fires outside their houses on October nights to keep off the tiny, stinging sandflies, she arranged on the night of 21 October 1959, when the moon was in the same phase as on 11 October 1492, to have brush fires kindled on High Cay, 114 feet above sea level, and at other high points on the east coast of San Salvador, which in 1492 was the most thickly populated section of the island. From the deck of a motorboat at 10 P.M., about 27 miles due east of High Cay, the fire was clearly visible over the western horizon, flaring up at intervals when the natives threw on more wood. The light died down when the natives retired, which explains why Columbus would see it flare up and then disappear.

About one hour after this sighting the moon rose, and at 2 A.M. Friday,

12 October, Rodrigo de Triana in *Pinta* cried, *"Tierra! Tierra!"* Land it was. The moonlight had kindled white the gray limestone cliffs of High Cay. Columbus, estimating it to be six or seven nautical miles to leeward, prudently ordered all sails but a reduced mainsail to be lowered, and jogged off and on until daylight to avoid the danger of possible reefs extending offshore. Mrs. Wolper's expedition sighted High Cay in the moonlight at 1:30 A.M., and our photograph of it by morning light (ii.2) is of dramatic interest as showing the first piece of the New World seen by any European since the voyages of the Northmen. There has been no change in the aspect of this land since 1492 — the same rough cliff topped by wind-blown bush, with a low, green island stretching northerly into the distance.

San Salvador, as Columbus named this island after Our Lord and Saviour, was known to the natives as Guanahaní. Fifteen to sixteen miles long and six to eight wide, it is surrounded by a breaking coral reef through which there are several passes on the south and west, but none on the east coast which Columbus first sighted. Since he was near the southeast point at daylight, he first sailed around the southern coast, looking for a gap in the reef.

ii.2

Wisely he did not attempt to thread the narrow channels which lead into a protected harbor behind High Cay, and into Sandy Point Harbor, which is also called French Bay (ii.3). He rounded Sandy Point, the southwestern cape of the island, and braced his yards up sharp for a run up the west coast. There, after about six miles of sailing, a break in the reef almost two miles wide was spotted by the masthead lookouts. The fleet came about on the port tack and steered cautiously under reduced sail toward a curving beach of coral sand. The bottom is visible in these waters at a depth of five to seven fathoms, and it was all clean sand and the water smooth under the lee of the land. So when it began to shoal beyond ten or twelve feet, Columbus fired a gun as the signal to anchor, the big iron hooks were dropped for the first time since Gomera, the rope cables paid out and secured, and the sails furled in such manner that they could be raised quickly if the natives appeared unfriendly.

Here (ii.4) took place the first New World landing of Columbus, the dramatic scene described by Las Casas and so often depicted by artists. On this broad white beach, bordered by green trees, Columbus stepped ashore from his barge and the two Captains Pinzón from their gigs. The royal standard of Castile and León and the fleet banners (on a white field a green cross with a crowned F for Ferdinand on the one arm and a crowned Y for Ysabel on the other) fluttered bravely in the fresh tradewind. "All hands, falling on their knees, with copious tears gave infinite thanks to Almighty God and Our Lord, who had brought them to a safe haven." Many of the landing party then knelt before Columbus, hailing him as Admiral of the

ii.4

Ocean Sea, Viceroy and Governor, and begging his forgiveness for having doubted his ability to sail west to the Indies. Columbus drew his sword and, pointing it toward Heaven, cried out, "I hereby take possession of this Island, to which I give the name San Salvador, in the name of the King and Queen my mighty sovereigns," pronouncing all their titles that he could remember, and commanding the wondering natives present to become their faithful subjects and vassals. The Indians, thought Las Casas, were more interested in the dress and appearance of these intruders, "being especially astonished at their beards and the fairness of their skin; and the Admiral, from the distinction and authority of his person, and also from the scarlet color of his costume, they guessed to be the chief man among them; and they reached out their hands to stroke the beards, marvelling at them since they had none, and even checking on hands and faces for their whiteness." Rodrigo de Escobedo, secretary of the fleet, and Sánchez de Segovia, the royal comptroller, recorded these proceedings on parchment, with inkhorn and quill pen, and doubtless supplied royal titles which Columbus could not remember.

The site of this ceremony, so significant for the entire future of the world, yet unchanged in aspect for almost five centuries, was unmarked by any monument until 1956, when Mrs. Wolper, with the coöperation of Pan American Airways personnel, erected on that beach a white cross (ii.5). It was dedicated on Christmas Day by the Reverend Nicholas Kremer O.S.B., and on the following Columbus Day it was visited by Don Cristobal Colón, Duke of Veragua, eighteenth generation in descent from Columbus himself.

ii.5

If further identification be needed, it can be furnished within a few hundred yards of the cross by what Columbus called "a quarry of stones naturally shaped very fair for church edifices or other royal works." Our photograph shows Morison sitting on some of these naturally squared coral blocks (ii.6). These squared stones are unique in the Bahamas, and the "many bodies of water, and a very big lake in the middle," mentioned by Columbus (ii.7), are by no means common. The lakes, fed by rain only, are brackish.

San Salvador in 1492 was thickly inhabited by people of the Arawak or Taino nation, whom Columbus promptly named Indians, assuming that he had arrived in "The Indies," and that Guanahaní was an island somewhere around Japan. The natives, having had plenty of time since daybreak to observe the Spanish ships, strange to them as today would be a missile from Mars, surrounded the landing party and paddled out to the ships in their

ii.6

dugout canoes. They offered no resistance and showed no fear, only wonder and curiosity. To the Spaniards the natives were "of good stature, very handsome people." They were not surprised to find their skin of the same brown color as the Canary Islanders', but were astonished by the Indians' unconscious nudity. "Some of the men wore scarves of cotton made like a mantilla . . . and the women wore in front a little thing of cotton which scarcely covered their pudenda." It was as if the golden age of man's innocence had here survived.

The natives overwhelmed them with gifts of live parrots, skeins of spun

cotton, and wooden spears tipped with stingray tails. They parted readily with their few golden nose-plugs for glass beads, red caps and especially *cascabeles* — the little spherical bells which were attached to trained hawks and falcons (ii.8). Hawk's bells were favored by Indians throughout the

Caribbean. Columbus tells of Indians approaching the ships in a canoe, wagging their fingers and saying, "*Chuque! Chuque!*" meaning, "Hawk's bells!" The San Salvadoreans made bread of corn and cassava, and from the island clay fashioned red pottery, many examples of which have been excavated under the direction of Ruth and Beatrice Wolper (ii.9).

The subsequent history of the Bahamian Arawaks, who showed Columbus and his men "as much love as if they were giving their hearts," is tragic. Spaniards, of whom Alonso de Hojeda in 1499 was possibly not the first, made a practice of raiding these islands for slaves. But they did not succeed in completely depopulating San Salvador, owing to a multitude of natural caves where people could conceal themselves, and to which the present natives still resort during hurricanes. Survivors amalgamated with Negroes brought in by the English in the eighteenth century. Many of the present-day Negroes show American Indian features, and all have preserved arts such as pounding corn into meal in a mortar fashioned from a hardwood tree trunk (ii.10), weaving baskets, and collecting piles of wood for their anti-sandfly fires.

ii.9

ii.10

In order to reconnoiter San Salvador, Columbus had himself rowed in *Santa María's* gig to the northern end of the island, in company with the caravels' barges. As they proceeded, Indians rushed down to the beach to offer gifts, or swam out to greet "the men who came from the sky," as they innocently called the Spaniards. In his boat Columbus entered the great reef-protected lagoon, now known as Graham's Harbor, which, with characteristic hyperbole, he said was "big enough to hold all the ships in Christendom." But he reported accurately that the entrance was "very narrow," and that within the harbor "the sea moves no more than within a well." It was a marvel to us that this harbor, measuring four to five miles each way and protected from the east, north and west winds only by five small cays and a submerged reef, should be so calm. Our first photograph (ii.11) of the southern half of Graham's Harbor, with the fresh-water lakes of San Salvador in the background, shows the contrast between the waves sweeping in from the ocean and the placid water inside. Rocky Point, as the peninsula is now called, was described by Columbus as "a piece of land which is formed like an island, although it isn't one . . . the which could in two days be made an island." The sea finally did just that, and the outer part of Columbus's peninsula, which he thought would be a good site for a fortress, is now an island called Cut Rock Cay. Our second photograph (ii.12) depicts White Cay at the northern apex of Graham's Harbor, with men investigating a wreck. Incidentally, the eastern shore of San Salvador is studded with wrecks of vessels whose captains

ii.11

were less fortunate, or less careful, than Columbus. Ironically, a Chicago newspaper in 1891 set up a monument above a breaker-swept spot on the eastern shore, close to one of those wrecks, inscribed "Columbus stepped ashore here."

In the subsequent history of San Salvador there are many gaps. Ponce de León called there in 1513, en route to the fountain of youth that he never located, to careen and cleanse the bottom of one of his ships. Las Casas called the island Triango, from its roughly triangular shape, taking White Cay as the apex; the English named it Watling's Island, after a pirate of whom little is known. At the outset of the nineteenth century, when interest in Columbus's landfall revived, stay-at-home historians squabbled as to whether Guanahaní was Watling's, Cat Island, Caicos, or half a dozen others. But the consensus, to which we subscribe, is that Guanahaní could not possibly be other than

ii.12

Watling's; and the British government placed its stamp of approval on this identification by officially renaming Watling's, San Salvador.

We now take leave of Guanahaní with a typical view of the western shore and the barrier reef (ii.13), between which Columbus was rowed to visit Graham's Harbor; and a conference of Obregón and Morison with hospitable Mrs. Wolper and her poodle Amour at her estate Polaris (ii.14).

ii.13

ii.14

CHAPTER III

On to Cathay

BEFORE leaving San Salvador, Columbus "took by force" several Indians, as he admitted in his letter to the Sovereigns, in order to use them as interpreters. "They soon understood us, and we them, either by speech or signs, and they have been very serviceable." These unwilling passengers, it may be presumed, could make nothing of the Spaniards' inquiries for the route to Catai (China) or Cipangu (Japan); but they easily guessed that gold rather than geography was their captors' major interest. Dwellers in the Bahamas obtained their few gold ornaments indirectly, by trading with Colba (Cuba), whose natives spoke their language. Wasn't this the big island which the Spaniards, making ample arm gestures and tracing Marco Polian outlines on deck, were seeking? So the Indians decided to guide the Admiral to "The Pearl of the Antilles" by their customary canoe route, one with the shortest crossings over open water. It ran from San Salvador to Rum Cay, Long Island, Crooked Island, the Ragged Islands and Cay Santo Domingo, whence the summits of Cuban mountains are visible on a clear day.

Columbus made sail late Sunday afternoon, after his boat visit to Graham's Harbor, and before sunset "saw so many islands that I could not decide where to go first." What he really saw was one island, looking like many separate ones because one can see its low hills thrusting up over the horizon at a greater distance than the intervening hollows. Our profile of this same island from a distance of 8 to 9 miles was sketched by Rudolf Cronau in 1890 (iii.1). The fleet hove-to for the night, for fear of encountering reefs, made sail at dawn 15 October, and around noon arrived at the now prosaically named

iii.1

Rum Cay, which the Admiral called Santa María de la Concepción. Columbus was usually systematic in his nomenclature. The first island discovered he named after the Saviour, the second after the Immaculate Conception, the third (Long Island) after the King, the fourth (Crooked Island) after the Queen, and the fifth after the Infante Don Juan, their heir.

Rum Cay resembles a miniature San Salvador. The fleet rounded the reef-fringed limestone bluff on the southeast end and anchored in St. George's Bay at the west end, where there is a big salt pond behind the land (iii.2). The impressed Indian guides told him that the natives here wore massy golden bracelets and anklets; but, as he remarked in his Journal, "All they said was humbug in order to escape," as two of them did. They jumped overboard and were picked up by a native canoe which was paddled so swiftly that no ship's boat could catch up with it; and the Indians, when pursued ashore, "fled like chickens." A little one-man canoe did come aboard the flagship, since its

iii.2

owner wished to see what a skein of cotton would bring in trade. Columbus paid a big price to gain good will — a red cap, a green glass bracelet, and two hawk's bells for earrings.

The building of *canoas*, which Columbus mentioned by name in his Journal and described as "little boats of a single tree without sail," is a lost art in the Bahamas, although they are still the most common small boat elsewhere in the Caribbean. In Panama we photographed a small dugout of the San Blas Indians, which must have been very similar to those seen by Columbus in 1492 (iii.3). The paddles are the same size and design as the stone carving of one which has been excavated at San Salvador (iii.4); thwarts and sternsheets are hand-hewn; fishlines and painter are of local fiber. Note the stone sinker, and the adze marks on the interior.

Rum Cay was unrewarding to Columbus, as it still is to yachtsmen. So on Monday morning, 16 October, when the wind backed to the southeast, rendering his anchorage dangerous, Columbus departed for the next island, where

iii.3

his guides again assured him that the natives wore an abundance of gold jewelry. This was Long Island, which the Admiral named Fernandina. En route he picked up another one-man canoe with its paddler, who offered the Admiral "some dry leaves which must be something much valued among them, since they had offered me some at San Salvador as a gift." Possibly these leaves were tobacco; but more likely they were dried leaves of various shrubs from which the modern natives of San Salvador brew an infusion which they find stimulating. Columbus used this Indian well, and set him ashore when he reached Long Island.

The wind was so light on Tuesday that the fleet had to lay-to all night, and made land after daybreak on Wednesday, 16 October. The Indian to whom Columbus had given the red cap and the hawk's bell earrings got there

iii.4

first, and both he and the owner of the tea leaves gave the Spaniards good advance publicity. When the fleet anchored off a village, a fleet of canoes set out, bearing "water and what they had." In return, Columbus presented them with brass tambourine jingles, lace-points, and some molasses, the taste of which must have astonished them, since there was no sugarcane as yet in the New World; all the Indians' sweetening came from honey.

Long Island is about sixty miles long and in most places only a mile or two wide. In 1492 it was covered with a thick growth of hardwood, but in the last century it has suffered from erosion, hurricanes and overgrazing, and today only the northern end corresponds to Columbus's extravagant praise. Here Columbus first noted in his Journal certain native products — a patch of cultivated maize which he called *panizo* (panic grass) (iii.5),[1] a tree so covered with parasites as to appear to grow leaves of several different species, and "fishes so unlike ours that it is marvelous . . . of the brightest colors in the world — blue, yellow, red, and of all colors, and the colors are so bright

[1] Our photograph, taken by the late Ernest G. Stillman in Cuba about 1930, shows the same type of corn that Columbus first encountered, growing in a native garden with cassava, and squash or pumpkin. The Indians had already in 1492 attained this high development of maize, of which specimens five thousand years old found in the Bat Caves of Mexico were only about an inch long. Information from Professor Paul C. Mangelsdorf.

iii.5

that there is no man who would not marvel and take great delight in seeing them." Our photograph (iii.6) of an apostolic haul of fish at nearby San Salvador may well represent what Columbus viewed. The fleet weighed anchor from off this hospitable village the same day that it arrived, and sailed northerly toward Cape Santa Maria (iii.7). Around this cape, nestling under its

iii.7

westerly hook, the Admiral discovered "a very wonderful harbor with . . . two mouths, for it has an island in the middle, and both are very narrow, and within it is wide enough for one hundred ships, if it [the bottom] were deep and clean and deep at the entrance." This must have been the harbor now called Hossie (iii.8), where a development company has established the Santa Maria Club. Columbus anchored outside, in Calabash Bay, but entered in a boat and landed. His description is very pleasing to the members of the club: "I walked among some trees, which were the most beautiful thing to see, . . . as much verdure as in the month of May in Andalusia, and all the trees were as different from ours as day from night; and so the herbage, the rocks, and all things." Some of his people entered the huts of friendly natives and saw their first Indian dogs, which to their amazement did not bark. The Indians bred them for eating, not hunting. The Spaniards found these *perros mudos*, dumb dogs, so palatable that within a century they were extinct.

iii.8

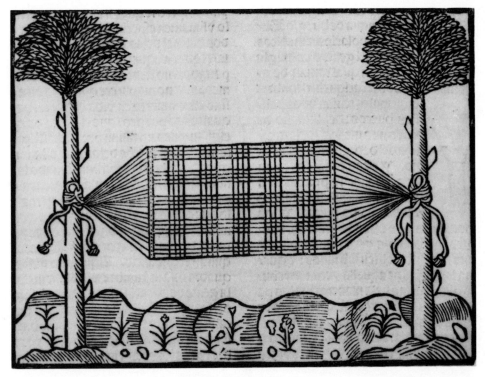

In each hut the Spaniards found a "bed and furnishings like nets of cotton." These, of course, were hammocks; the name *hamaca* is first used by Columbus in his Journal (3 November). Our illustration (iii.9) from Oviedo's *Historia* of 1535 is probably the earliest attempt of a European to depict one. Here was an Arawak invention that Europeans found a bonanza, both for comfort in a hot climate and for economy in space. Sailors of every European nation were shortly to be issued hammocks instead of having to seek out a "soft plank" as bed; only recently has the hammock been replaced by bunks and mattresses in the British and United States navies. And in North America the hammock, slung on a shady piazza or between two trees, was the favorite place for rest and amorous dalliance when your senior author was young and still is in your junior author's country.

Columbus ascertaining the west side of Long Island to be foul ground, studded with coral heads, the fleet doubled Cape Santa Maria again, and by daylight 18 October, after passing a cliffy part of the coast now called Burnt Ground, reached a little harbor near the south cape of the island (iii.10), and anchored off it for the night. Long Island had been another disappointment as to gold; the Spaniards found only one bit of it, a nose stud on a native who refused to trade. But the impressed guides assured them that another island to

iii.10

the eastward, which they called Saomete, was a real gold mine. So, on Friday the 19th Columbus, in order not to miss this island, ordered his fleet to fan out until noon, when *Pinta* and *Niña* should close the flagship. *Santa María* at about 9 A.M. sighted the island, which the Admiral named Isabela. It is now called Crooked Island, and the deep water (over 1200 fathoms in most places) which the fleet crossed that day is the much frequented Crooked Island Passage.

By noon all three ships had reached "the north point, where there's an inlet and a rocky reef making out to it from the north, and another between it and the big island." The islet, on which there is now a tall lighthouse, is called

Bird Rock; and the harbor behind it, Portland Harbor (iii.11). Thence the fleet turned south and anchored for the night off the cape of Fortune Island, which Columbus named Cabo Hermoso (iii.12). It is anything but beautiful to-day — a flat expanse of scrub above dark Aeolian limestone cliffs — but, as with so many other Bahamian islands devastated by man and nature, Fortuna Island may then have been covered by fine timber. The Admiral adds, "Approaching this cape, there came so fair and sweet a smell of flowers or trees from the land, that it was the sweetest thing in the world." That, we can testify, was no exaggeration, for when the *Mary Otis* lay-to in the lee of Crooked Island on the night of 10 June 1940, the tradewind wafted delicious odors to us from the land. Columbus also noted between Fortune and Crooked

iii.11

Islands a great lagoon, now called the Bight of Acklins. The entrance is split three ways by the Rat and Goat Cays (iii.13).

That was on 20 October. Columbus tried to enter the Bight but found it too full of coral heads for safety, so doubled back, and at 10 A.M. Sunday the 21st anchored in Portland Harbor behind Bird Rock. There he went ashore in search of a "king" who, according to the Indian guides, went clothed, and

"wears ever so much gold"; but no such person was to be found. The people killed a big iguana (iii.14), and saved the skin to show the Sovereigns; and Columbus spotted some specimens of the native century plant (*Agave bahamana trelease*), which he thought to be *liñaloe*, medicinal aloes. It was a nat-

iii.14

ural mistake, as may be seen from our photograph of *Aloe vera*, introduced from Asia, in the Harvard Botanical Garden at Soledad, Cuba (iii.15). The aloe, Columbus had read in Marco Polo, was one of the leading staples of southeast China, so he caused quantities of the handsome but medicinally valueless plant agave to be gathered (iii.16). The natives here fled when they saw the Spaniards, but a few made bold to approach, and were given beads and hawk's bells in return for helping to fill water casks. Next day others brought skeins of cotton to swap for beads, and gladly exchanged gold noseplugs for hawk's bells.

iii.16

iii.15

After a spell of calm, the fleet weighed at midnight to resume what the Indian guides correctly insisted to be the route to Cuba, and which Columbus hoped to be the road to Japan. They recrossed Crooked Island Passage in a very light wind, sighting far distant the southern Cape Verde of Long Island, and on the afternoon of 25 October saw "seven or eight islands all strung out, north to south." These were the Ragged Cays, a long line of islands and reefs that tail off from the Great Bahama Bank. Columbus called them Islas de Arena, Isles of Sand. The fleet anchored for the night of 26 October off Great Ragged Island, southernmost of the group (iii.17), from which the guides assured the Admiral it was but a day and a half's journey by canoe to Cuba. And, "because of the signs that the Indians made of its greatness and of its gold and pearls," Columbus felt sure that he was approaching Japan.

At sunrise 27 October the fleet got under way from its last anchorage in the Bahamas. Crossing a wide expanse of shoal water, colored deep blue, emerald and purple by the coral and weeds below, they sighted before nightfall the

iii.17

tiny Cay Santo Domingo (iii.18) and the mountains of Cuba, and lay-to for the night.

Before this First Voyage was completed, Martín Alonso Pinzón visited Great Inagua. The fleet had heard about that island in Cuba. The Indian guides, following their usual method of arousing curiosity about the next island, said that in Babeque, as they called it, the natives "gathered gold on the beach by candles at night, and then made bars of it with a hammer." Columbus tried to follow their sailing directions thither, but encountered headwinds and gave it up. Pinzón, however, was so enamored of this golden fable that he sailed *Pinta* away from the fleet on 21 November and gave himself plenty of time to explore Great Inagua before rejoining the Admiral six weeks later. Of course he found the story to be completely false; the Great Inaguans had no gold to pick up by candle or any other light.

In modern times the owners of this big island (iii.19) have acquired gold indirectly through evaporating salt from seawater. The contrast of the red salt pans with white coral beaches and blue, green and purple shoals outside is most striking. Unfortunately, the salt pans are also great mosquito breeders, and in 1963 such swarms of mosquitoes settled on the crew of Six-zero-Papa when they came down on the Great Inagua landing strip that they hastily re-fueled and took off, without checking on the alleged gold.

Columbus never returned to the Bahamas; and Spain showed no interest in Los Lucayos, as they called them,[1] except as a source of kidnapped Indian slave labor; the Greater Antilles were so much more profitable. The first European settlers, in the seventeenth century, were English; and by the end of the next century the Bahamas, reinforced by British loyalists and their slaves from the continent, became the scene of flourishing sugar plantations.

[1] Las Casas says that the people of the Bahamas called themselves "*los Lucayos,* i.e., dwellers on cays, *cayos* being their word for those small islands."

iii.19

iv.1

CHAPTER IV

Cuba

THE Harvard Columbus Expedition's Cuban cruise took place in June and July of 1940 in the 45-foot ketch *Mary Otis* (iv.1) owned and skippered by William D. Stevens, with Albert Harkness, Jr., Enos Verge, and Morison as crew. *Mary Otis*, designed by Stevens himself and built at South Bristol, Maine, had already made one round trip to Cuba and two round voyages across the Atlantic. She proved an ideal yacht for our purpose, with a congenial crew. Stevens was one of America's ablest blue-water Corinthians; Verge was a Maine shellback with fifty years' experience under sail; and Harkness, a student of Latin American history, entered the foreign service and at the time of writing is cultural attaché to the American Embassy at Santiago de Chile.

We approached Cuba as Columbus had done, via the Ragged Islands and Cay Santo Domingo, and, following the course indicated in his Journal, hit Bahía Bariay exactly as he did. Since (as explained in the Introduction) aircraft Six-zero-Papa was unable to fly along those Cuban coasts — except around Cape Maisí and to Guantánamo — the illustrations of scenery in this chapter are snapshots taken in 1940, or photographs furnished by our Cuban friends, or by the United States Navy. The trees and plants were photographed by Mr. Crofoot at the tropical garden of the University of the West Indies, Trinidad, in the course of our 1963 flight in Six-zero-Papa.

Santa María, *Pinta* and *Niña* entered Bahía Bariay on 28 October 1492. The landmark, as he noted in his Journal, was a range of mountains which reminded him of the Peña de los Enamorados near Granada (Robert Southey's "Lovers' Rock"), the most conspicuous having on its summit "another little peak like a pretty little mosque" (iv.2). It is now called La Teta de Bariay.

[45]

iv.2

They entered this small, deep harbor, anchored, and Columbus went into rap-
tures over the beauty of the place: "It was a great pleasure to see those green
things and groves of trees and to hear the birds sing." He noted especially
the *ruiseñores*, nightingales; these were doubtless the Hispaniola mockingbird.
He observed the thatch palm (iv.3) with which the natives walled and roofed

iv.3

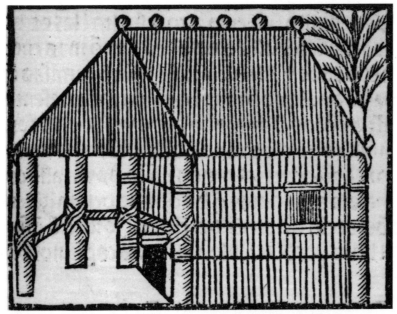

their houses — and do to this day — and noted that the *bohíos* (huts) looked like Moorish tents; i.e., tents with ridgepoles (iv.4). Among other products he reported purslane and amaranth (iv.5). He tarried there only one night, and on the 29th sailed a short leg westward to Puerto Gibara, which he named Río de Mares.

iv.5

Puerto Gibara, where Columbus spent about two weeks, and which he correctly predicted would become an important place for trade, is marked, he said, by "two somewhat rounded mountains." These, now called La Silla (Saddle) de Gibara, are seen in our view from the shore of the harbor (iv.6).

iv.6

Since the San Salvador guides assured the local Indians that they had nothing to fear from their visitors, Columbus had no trouble making friends. He made a point of gathering fruits and plants that he hoped would prove valuable, as well as evidence of being in the Indies: *Canella alba,* which smelled like cinnamon but wasn't cinnamon; *Pimenta dioica,* the allspice or creole pepper (iv.7), sweet potatoes (or yams), several varieties of beans and of wild cotton, "and a thousand kinds of fruit that I can't describe." But, although Columbus was assured by "yessing" Indians that he was only a few hundred miles from Marco Polo's "noble city of Zaitun" (Changchow) and Quinsay (Hangchow), the "city of Heaven," he could not find anything remotely resembling what Marco Polo described. No multitudes of people, horses and donkeys; no marble bridges with commoners kowtowing to mandarins in rich costumes; no courtesans with faces like white eggs, carried in palanquins; no sword-girt Samurai. Nothing but smelly, palm-thatched *bohíos,* and naked Arawaks who were friendly but had nothing to offer.

[48]

Whenever Columbus mentioned *El Gran Can*, describing in dumb show a great prince, local Indians pointed inland toward the place where their cacique resided. Columbus jumped to the conclusion that this was an important Chinese proconsul, if not the emperor himself, and with pathetic punctilio organized an "embassy" thither. Luis de Torres, the fleet interpreter, headed this mission because (a converted Jew) he knew Hebrew and Arabic, which it was assumed would enable him to converse with the Chinese; his colleague was Rodrigo de Jerez, an able seaman chosen because he had once called on a local "king" in Africa and so was supposed to know how to approach royalty. They had an Indian guide and a porter to carry gifts, and the fleet's official papers — Latin passport and letter of credence from the Sovereigns.

The embassy followed an Indian trail up the beautiful Cacoyuguin valley, and we followed them as far as we could by boat with our Gibara guides — Dr. Joaquin de la Vara, and the captain of the port (iv.8). In two days the

iv.8

embassy reached an important village near the present town of Holguin; we, transferring from boat to car, were there within an hour. The Spaniards were received "with great solemnity," and seated in the cacique's "palace" on carved Arawak ceremonial stools, where they were feasted by the cacique, and their hands and feet were kissed by the common people. Ferdinand, the Admiral's son, described these *dujos*, as the Spaniards learned they were called, as "seats made of one piece . . . like some animal with short arms and legs, the tail lifted up to lean against, and a head at the other end, with golden eyes and ears." We show a good example of a ceremonial *dujo* answering Ferdinand's description, from the British Museum (iv.9).

A glorious time was had by the "ambassadors"; one can imagine Rodrigo telling his shipmates, "I never had it so good"! But their report was a terrible disappointment to Columbus.

He little guessed the importance of something they did see. On their return down this beautiful valley, they met "many people who were going to their villages . . . with a firebrand in the hand and herbs to drink the smoke thereof, as they are accustomed." This is the first mention in history of smoking tobacco. The word *tobaco*, in Arawak, means cigar, which is the way they used it — inserting one end of the rolled and wrapped leaf in a nostril, they applied a firebrand to the other end, inhaled the smoke a few times, then passed it to a friend. Some forty years elapsed before Spaniards generally began to smoke tobacco; its use then spread over Europe, Asia and Africa with remarkable celerity, and became more pervasive than any religion.

iv.9

During the embassy's absence, Columbus had his ships careened, one at a time, and their bottoms cleansed of weed and barnacles, on a beach within Puerto Gibara which the Cubans were still using in 1939 for the same purpose. The rocky western point of the harbor, Columbus remarked, would be a good place for a fort; and over three centuries later Spain built Morro Fernando VII. Bartolomé García, *Niña*'s boatswain, now claimed a reward because he had, so he thought, discovered a tree of gum mastic, which Columbus knew from his early voyages to Chios to be a valuable source of resin. What Bartolomé actually saw was *Bursera simaruba*, locally called the gumbo-limbo, bearing a berry which, when crushed, smells like varnish (iv. 10). Anyway (so a local Arawak told him by signs), the mastic was good for the stomach-ache.

[51]

iv.10

Columbus's stay at Puerto Gibara was broken by a short trip westward. He noted Punta Uvero's majestic royal palms, whose descendants are growing there today. He got as far as Punta Covarubia, from which a later Spaniard took the title of count, and whose descendants still own it. He missed the narrow entrance to Puerto Padre and turned back to Puerto Gibara because the wind, unseasonably, backed to the westward.

On 12 November 1492 the fleet made its final departure from Puerto Gibara and by sunset was off Punta Lucrecia (iv.11), which the Admiral named Cabo de Cuba because he supposed it to be the eastern promontory of the island. The shores around Bahía Nipe were invisible, and the high mountains beyond he assumed to belong to another island. They stood off-and-on that night, sailed eastward on the 13th; then (as the wind headed them) south and

iv.11

west, and entered Bahía Tánamo, which Columbus named La Mar de Nuestra Señora, the Sea of Our Lady; and the harbor, Puerto del Principe, obviously after the Infante Don Juan. Here he raised a cross.

iv.12

Bahía Tánamo itself (iv.12) is little changed since Columbus's visit. He spent four days there, explored it in his barge, and praised "the fertility and beauty of the islands in this harbor . . . some of which seem to reach the sky, and were shaped like diamond points; others have at the greatest point a top like a table, . . . all full of trees." (iv.13) Barring exaggeration (the tallest island rises only to 250 feet), this is a good description of Tánamo Bay.

iv.13

Some of these islands, said Columbus, "were cultivated with the roots from which the Indians make their bread." This, of course, was the manioc or cassava, a source of bread that the Spaniards learned to appreciate even more than maize, and which eventually spread world-wide. It was also at Tánamo that Columbus first saw what he called *nueces de India,* the coconut mentioned but not described by Marco Polo. Actually, the coconut palm had not reached the Caribbean in 1492. What Columbus took to be it was *Chrysobalanus icaco,* locally called icaco, whose small fruit is edible but far from palatable. Our engraving of it (iv.14) is from a French *Histoire des Antilles* of 1658. Columbus also reported "an infinite amount of aloes." These were some variety of agave, probably not the same as the one he had seen in the Bahamas.

iv.14

For several days the fleet tacked eastward against light airs. In the meantime, Martín Alonso Pinzón, possibly exasperated by the Admiral's slow speed and bemused by the Indians' tall tales of gold, squared away for Great Inagua Island (see previous chapter).

The next harbor that *Santa María* and *Niña* made was Puerto Cayo Moa, which the Admiral named Santa Catalina, probably as a compliment to the seven-year-old Spanish Infanta who became the first wife of Henry VIII of England; in any case it was the feast day of St. Catherine the virgin martyr. One enters this harbor through a gap in a long breaking reef, the Cayo Moa Grande; once inside, you are in a great protected bay over eight miles long and one and a half wide, with a least depth of six fathoms, bordered on the land side by a noble sierra clad with the Cuban pine, and down which a mountain stream tumbles and roars, then quiets down (iv.15) as though to match the calm bay. Columbus caused a new pine mizzen mast and yard to be cut and trimmed for *Niña*, and correctly predicted that sawmills would eventually be built up the river. He went into ecstasies over the peculiar beauty of this great harbor, so placid between the austere mountains and the hissing barrier reef. When we visited Puerto Cayo Moa in 1940 (iv.16) it was still clean of human touch, but a factory has since been established on its shores.

iv.16

On 26-27 November the Spaniards weathered Punta Plata, which they named Cabo Campana, and noted five or six good harbors under their lee; for Oriente Province is as richly provided with harbors as the coast of Maine. This part of Cuba is incredibly beautiful — tumbled mountains and constantly changing cloud effects, palm-covered green hills bordering the sea, with a wreath of white breakers at their feet, vegetation lush and brilliant, harbors many and fully protected.

The next landmark that Columbus sighted, and a familiar one to sailors ever since, was El Yunque (The Anvil), rising over 1900 feet directly from the sea to a tabletop (iv.17). He could already see Cape Maisí, the easternmost extremity of Cuba, but was diverted by "a very singular harbor" shaped

iv.17

iv.18

"like a little porringer (*escodilla*)." That was Baracoa. As our aërial photograph of 1954 proves, the porringer shape is exact (iv.18), and the Buren Rock, which the Admiral observed off Punta Barlovento, the eastern point (iv.19), is still a danger to navigation. The Río Macaguanigua, whose old mouth (in the center) Columbus's barge was able to enter directly, has since built up a bar at that point and runs halfway around the harbor's rim before finding an outlet. Baracoa is another place for which Columbus predicted great things. The first Spanish settlement in Cuba was made there in 1510, and it is now an important center for banana export.

iv.19

Santa María and *Niña*, windbound, stayed there several days, without seeing any natives — all fled, thinking that the Spaniards were raiding Caribs. Columbus took advantage of the delay to erect a cross on Punta Barlovento and probably for that reason named the harbor Puerto Santo. What purports to be the actual cross — it may well be, since Spain founded the town of Baracoa less than twenty years later — was shown to us in the cathedral in 1940. We were told that every year it mysteriously disappears but is always found on the point where Columbus originally erected it.

The Admiral took the opportunity to visit the nearby Playa Miel (Honey Beach), where there was a big lagoon — since silted up — and where he

iv.20

first made friendly contact with the Arawaks of this region. They cultivated maize, gourds and pumpkins, lived in beehive-shaped, palm-thatched huts separated by partitions, and possessed enormous dugout canoes; one, said Columbus, could hold 150 people. No tree of that size exists in Cuba today; but the big tree on the right of our photograph taken at the Harvard Botanical Garden at Soledad is a ceiba, or silk-cotton tree, the Indians' favorite for dugout construction; this one would make a 20-man canoe. The tree in the center is a native cabbage palm (iv.20). The Miel is a beautiful river, bordered by groves of royal palms (iv.21); above them one can see in our photo the curiously shaped mountain summit which later Spaniards ungallantly named La Teta de María Teresa, after a corpulent and fecund empress.

On 4 December Columbus weighed from Baracoa, sailed eastward with a fair wind, sounded from his barge Puerto Boma, and observed the entrances to Puerto Mata and the Río Yumurí, a narrow gorge looking like a butcher's cleaver slice in the escarpment (iv.22). That night he spent hove-to off

Punta del Fraile (which he called Cabo Lindo), the northern bulge of Cape
Maisí. At sunrise on the 5th, the point of Cape Maisí was in view. Here is its
profile as it appeared to us in *Mary Otis* in the light of a full moon, which kindled the tradewind clouds to bright silver (iv.23); a night at sea memorable
for its transcendent beauty, as we doubled the cape under mainsail and spinnaker. Cape Maisí today is topped by a complex which very much looks like
sites for guided missiles. (iv.24).

iv.24

Before rounding this cape to follow Columbus on his later exploration of southern Cuba, we wish to show (iv.25) the genial features of the late Brother León of the Colegio La Salle, and of Dr. J. P. Carabia, another eminent Cuban botanist, who identified Columbus's Cuban flora for us at Havana.

iv.25

Columbus returned to Cape Maisí on 29 April 1494, at the beginning of his exploration of the south coast, and there landed to erect a cross and reassert Spanish dominion. It was then that he named it Cabo Alfa y Omega, Cape Alpha and Omega, because he had decided that Cuba was not an island but a promontory of China, and that this cape was the beginning of the East and the end of the West. Andrés Bernáldez, the chronicler of Ferdinand and Isabella, who obtained his information orally from Columbus two years later, was bemused by the thought that one might start walking westward from

Cape Maisí and eventually reach Cape St. Vincent in Portugal, "without crossing any part of the Ocean Sea," and that the entire population of the world was contained between these two capes. Columbus never abandoned his belief that Cuba was the Chinese province of Mangi, and that Zaitun and Quinsay were just around the corner.

The fleet on this part of Columbus's Second Voyage consisted of well-tried *Niña* and two smaller caravels, *San Juan* and *Cardera*, with a total complement of about sixty officers and men. The Admiral's journal for this voyage has disappeared, but we have detailed accounts by his Genoese friend and shipmate Michele de Cuneo, and by Bernáldez. Peter Martyr, the earliest historian of the New World, also obtained a few details from Columbus.

The Admiral found a very different terrain south and west of Cape Maisí from what he had seen in 1492 west and north of it. Here was an ironbound coast consisting of a series of limestone escarpments, backed by a sierra that rises to 4000 feet above the ocean. This coast of Oriente Province is arid, but far from barren. Passing Punta Calita and Punta la Llana (iv.26) on the last day of April, "There were wafted out to sea very delicate perfumes," says

iv.26

iv.27

Peter Martyr; doubtless that of the sea grape, which was then at its most fragrant (iv.27), and of the flowers of the cactus which lines this coast of Cuba (iv.28). As we followed this course in *Mary Otis*, delicious odors came out to us in the dawn watch, recalling the superb lines of José-María de Heredia on the *arôme subtil* that he remembered from his native shores of Cuba. But all we got in Six-zero-Papa was the exhaust from the jet planes that the Navy kindly sent out to escort us.

iv.28

Fifty miles from Cape Maisí the fleet found its first harbor on the south coast, which Peter Martyr described as "in the form of a sickle, shut in on both sides by promontories that break the waves; large and very deep" (iv. 29). Upon entering, it opened up into a great bay which Columbus named Puerto Grande. This was Guantánamo Bay, on whose shores the United States maintains a great naval station.

Just inside the entrance the Spaniards landed, and were lucky to find friendly Arawaks preparing a sumptuous picnic of fish and iguana to feast a neighboring cacique whom they expected shortly. The fish they cooked by placing them in a split green log, balancing the log on two rocks, and building a fire below; by the time the wood was consumed the fish was roasted to a turn. The visitors helped themselves to roast fish, distributing the usual hawk's bells and beads in payment, but would accept no iguana. For that the Indians were grateful, because these reptiles were difficult to catch, and it would have gone hard with them had they failed to supply the cacique with his anticipated *plat du jour*.

iv.29

Leaving Guantánamo Bay before sunrise May Day, the fleet ranged this rugged coast westward, sailing close to shore as there were no outlying reefs. At certain points, like Daiquiri, there was a narrow, cultivated and thickly inhabited plain on the edge of the sea (iv.30). Multitudes of Indians paddled out in canoes, offering cassava bread and calabashes of sweet water, and crying in their language, "Eat and drink, men from the sky!" The fleet passed the site of Siboney where the American expeditionary force landed in 1898, and then found a break in the sierra where a narrow channel leads between rocky headlands into the great bay of Santiago de Cuba, which Columbus named Puerto del Rey (iv.31). Here were cultivated fields and multitudes of Indians, many of whom paddled out to the caravels with offerings of fish, cassava bread and water. Departing at dawn 2 May, the caravels next day, festival of the Discovery of the True Cross, were off a high cape which Columbus appropriately named Cabo Cruz. It is still so called; the only name given by Columbus to any part of Cuba which has survived; but Cape Cruz is curiously elusive to photographers — we rounded it before daylight, and a poor sketch from an old *Sailing Directions for the West Indies* (iv.32) is the best that we can offer.

[65]

iv.31

As the coast trends northeasterly from this cape, Columbus chose to leave Cuba temporarily for an excursion to Jamaica, where the Indians assured him he really would find gold. This trip we shall discuss in Chapter XI. Back off Cape Cruz two weeks later, he began a long, tedious sail around the Gulf of Guacanayabo. Here he became involved in an archipelago of tiny islets which he named El Jardín de la Reina, the Queen's Garden. It is now called El Laberinto de las Doce Leguas. The islets, and Columbus counted 164 in one day, were "all green and full of trees, the fairest that eyes beheld. Some were covered with royal palms, others with calabash trees as large as one of our

Pico Turquino (bearing 060°, distant about 64 miles)

iv.32   CABO CRUZ FROM WESTWARD

iv.33

elms." This was *Crescentia cujete*, the bottle-gourd from whose fruit the Indians made their cooking and drinking vessels (iv.33). But time has not dealt kindly with the Queen's Garden. The trees have been pushed out by mangroves, the mangroves were killed in 1932 by a hurricane, and in 1940, instead of fair islets, we beheld cays covered with bare, bristly dead limbs (iv.34)). We were glad to escape through the Laberinto de las Doce Leguas, as Columbus eventually did, to deep water. But our admiration for Columbus's

iv.34

ability to find his way safely through intricate channels and shoal waters was unbounded. Outside the Laberinto we set the spinnaker (iv.35) and bowled along until the usual evening thunderstorm blew up. Columbus reported that the thunderstorms of this coast were the worst he had ever experienced, and we say that too; *Mary Otis* narrowly escaped losing her sails, and Obregón once flew into a thunderstorm so bad that he was forced to land at Camagüey without papers.

From Cayo Bretón, marking the western end of the Laberinto, Columbus shaped a course toward lofty mountains that he sighted to the northwest. This was the Sierra de Trinidad (iv.36). Cautiously approaching this coast to avoid outlying reefs, he lay-to during a night memorable for sweet odors from the land; next day, Whitsunday, he entered the mouth of the San Juan river. Columbus named it El Río de las Misas because the fleet chaplain here

said the first mass ever celebrated in Cuba. Numerous Indians, attracted by curiosity over this strange ceremony, came forward with gifts of pigeons and native products. An aged man amoung them, quaintly described by Peter Martyr as "respectable though naked," addressed to the Admiral a long welcoming speech which Diego Colón, the interpreter, translated into Castilian and Peter Martyr converted into not very convincing Latin, as he makes the old boy discuss the immortality of the soul. Diego was the baptismal name of this Indian, who was taken from San Salvador on the First Voyage and became an indispensable interpreter on the Second.

Now the fleet cut away from the coast and so missed the great Bahía Jagua, where the city of Cienfuegos is located. The next bay that it entered was the Golfo de Cochinos, which in 1961 acquired sad notoriety under the literal translation "Bay of Pigs." Here, Columbus told Bernáldez, "On the edge of the sea, close by a great grove of palms that seemed to reach the sky, there gushed forth two springs of water below . . . and when the tide was on the flood, the water was so cold and of such goodness and so sweet, that no better could be found in the world . . . and all rested there on the grass by those springs amid the scent of the flowers which was marvelous, and the sweetness of the singing of little birds, so many and so delightful, and under the shade of those palms so tall and fair that it was a wonder to see it all." The subterranean springs are still there (iv.37), indicated by the dark spot in the water, welling up sweet water into the salt. Here comes the mirage-eyed manatee (which Columbus called *sirena*, mermaid), to drink her fill, and seamen can obtain drinking water without going ashore.

Not far away they marveled at flocks of pink flamingoes and enjoyed watching local Indians catch turtles with a tame remora, the sucking fish. They would cast the little fellow adrift from a canoe, with a line attached to his tail, not failing to urge him to "be of good courage, my friend." Fishie attached his sucker-head to turtle's carapace so firmly that he could be reeled in, complete with turtle. When the prey was gaffed, fishie was politely requested to let go, and then rewarded with some bits of the meat.

Passing Golfo Cazones, the fleet left the blue deeps and entered what the 1885 *Sailing Directions for the West Indies* calls "the White Grounds." They are white because the bottom is of marl; Columbus said it was like sailing in a sea of milk. Suddenly the water looked like ink, where the bottom of fine

iv.37

black sand was stirred up by the waves. These phenomena, and the story of the sucking fish, caused Columbus to be branded by many as a liar when he returned home. Spaniards were ready to believe stories of people with tails or with eyes in the middle of the breast, as they had read as much in Sir John Mandeville; but the Admiral's stories were incredible! It was like the case of the Yankee sailor who, when asked what he had seen in the West Indies, said, "Mountains of sugar, rivers of rum, and fish that fly in the air." People believed the first two, but flying fish, never — that was "unnatural"!

Columbus anchored under one of the Cayos Providencias, whence he sent a small caravel to the Cuban shore in search of fresh water, the weather having turned so hot that they were in danger of going dry. The men reported that on this part of the Zapata Peninsula the mangrove bushes and roots, "so thick that a cat couldn't get ashore," were as strong a deterrent as a wall — a very apt description (iv.38). So the Admiral sailed on, naming the end of the

iv.38

peninsula Punta del Serafín because it was 27 May, the Feast of Angels. Crossing the Ensenada Broa, they anchored off a palm grove near the present town of Batabanó. Thence they fairly crawled along the north shore of the gulf, often having to kedge *Niña* through a muddy shoal by planting an anchor ahead and all hands heaving on the windlass. But the Gulf was not devoid of interest and amusement; they encountered so vast a flotilla of turtles that the shells rattled against the ships' topsides; they gathered conch shells with savory meat inside "as big as a man's arm"; and mammoth oysters which yielded no pearls but were "very good eating," and "crayfish without end."

It was now mid-June, the fleet had reached Bahía Cortés where the land trends southward, and Diego the interpreter could no longer understand the natives. These were the Siboney, whom the Arawaks had chased into the western end of Cuba. Something had to be done, for provisions were running short. The men were surfeited with cassava bread and seafood, grumbling over the labor of kedging through shallows, and fearful of never getting home. The caravels were leaking, strained by frequent grounding, and their rigging was going rotten. So the Admiral decided to give up his quest for proof that Cuba was China, and an even wilder project, to sail home around the world. In order to save himself from blame for a premature return, and on the precedent of what Bartholomew Dias did in 1488 when forced to give up his quest for India, Columbus had the fleet secretary draft a declaration to the effect that all hands were satisfied with Cuba being an Asiatic peninsula and no island. Almost everyone on board the three caravels signed; but Juan de la Cosa later reneged and depicted Cuba fairly correctly on his famous *mappemonde* dated 1500.

Turning back from Bahía Cortés, the fleet began a long and arduous beat to windward. Five weeks were required to reach Cape Cruz, whence Columbus turned south to circumnavigate Jamaica. He saw Cuba only twice again. On the outward passage of his Fourth Voyage in the summer of 1502, he took off from one of the cays, possibly Cayo Largo, for the Bay Islands, Honduras; and in May 1503, after crossing the Caribbean from the Gulf of Darien, his two remaining caravels found shelter in the narrow, rocky harbor formed by Cayo Cinco Balas and Cayo Bretón. There they rode out a severe gale and lost all but one of their anchors, whose cable parted, all but one strand. Thence they struggled to windward to a harbor east of Cape Cruz, probably Puerto Pilón. The rugged Sierra Maestra (iv.39), seen over the stern of worm-eaten caravel *Capitana*, was the last that Columbus saw of this "Pearl of the Antilles."

iv.39

CHAPTER V

Hispaniola

HISPANIOLA was honored by Columbus with the name "The Spanish Isle." Here he established his first garrison, built his first colonial town, as well as Santo Domingo, the capital today; and here he spent the major part of his time ashore in the West Indies. From Hispaniola he derived the most profit, but experienced his deepest frustrations: a flagship lost, Navidad destroyed, two rebellions, wars with the natives, imprisonment at the hands of a royal agent, and the humiliation of being forbidden to enter the principal harbor to take refuge from a hurricane.

This great and beautiful island, now divided between the Haitian and Dominican republics, was not discovered by Columbus, although he received the credit. Martín Alonso Pinzón in *Pinta* got there first, on or about 1 December 1492, after ascertaining that no gold was to be obtained in Great Inagua. He ranged the north coast ahead of the flagship and *Niña*, and rejoined the caravel at Monte Cristi in time to sail home in company.

Columbus reached Hispaniola about a week later than did Pinzón. Crossing the Windward Passage from Cuba on the night of 5-6 December 1492, at dawn he was within sight of the cape and harbor that he named San Nicolás, because it was the feast of "Santa Claus," the patron saint of children. At the hour of vespers he entered the great harbor which is still called Port Saint Nicolas Môle. He "marveled at its beauty and graciousness, and although he had given great praise to the harbors of Cuba, he says that without doubt this is . . . surpassing them."

Our air photograph (v.1) taken from the northeastward, shows the *carénage* or inner harbor across the isthmus which separates it from the ocean and where, as Columbus noted, "The depth is 11 fathoms and all mud or clear sand," so deep even near shore that a ship could lay "alongside the grass." Just

over the low cape on the right (Cap Saint Nicolas Môle), one can see the main entrance to the harbor; beyond is the high Cap Foux which Columbus called Cabo de la Estrella, of the Star.

The Admiral landed on a fine beach and admired the ilex and other trees, but his prediction that this port would be a great center of world commerce has never been fulfilled. The surrounding country is too arid and unfruitful for sugarcane, and no valuable hardwoods grow nearby. The harbor did become a favorite anchorage of the Royal Navy during the Napoleonic wars, and there have been proposals to make it a British, German, or United States naval base; but the British preferred Port Royal, Jamaica, and the Americans, Guantánamo. The vast harbor is now empty of shipping, and its shores are deserted except for a small village of poor fishermen.

This and all the northern part of the Haitian coast was reconnoitered by Morison in 1939 on board *Chaloupe No. 5* of the Haitian Navy. She is here seen (v.2), fitting for sea at Port-au-Prince under the benevolent gaze of the Right Reverend Harry R. Carson, Bishop of Haiti. In this vessel all the cooking (and, I suspect the washing, too) was done in one pot over a charcoal fire in a deck box; but the freshly roasted and mortar-ground mountain coffee

V.2

made therein, with which the lieutenant commanding and the historian were awakened on a cold January dawn in Port Saint Nicolas Môle, was delicious beyond compare.

From that harbor Columbus rounded the cape and, with a fortunate southwest wind, ranged the arid, ironbound coast of northwest Haiti, which the French call Les Côtes de Fer. It is broken only by a gorge which Columbus called *un'agrezuela* (Journal, 7 December), and which we photographed in 1963 (v.3) when the river bed was dry.

Here we venture to reproduce a page from Morison's field notebook of 1939 (v.4), showing the northern coast of Haiti sketched from off Pointe Jean Rabel, a point which Columbus, on 6 December 1492, named Cabo Cinquin. He named the next prominent cape eastward Cabo del Elefante. This cape (Grande Pointe on the modern chart), when viewed as a continuation

of the Haut Piton mountain, does somewhat resemble a huge elephant coming down to Tortuga Channel to drink. The island of Tortuga (v.5) was so called by Columbus because of its obvious resemblance to a turtle basking on the surface.

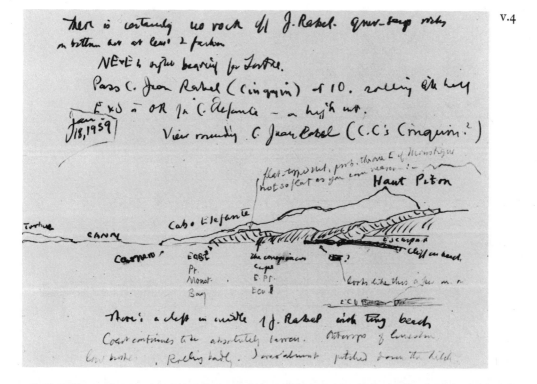

Noting, as he passed, the modern Port à l'Ecu, Columbus entered on 7 December 1492 a harbor that he called Puerto de la Concepción because it was the vigil of Our Lady's Conception (v.6). Here *Santa María* and *Niña* lay windbound for several days. The seamen caught fishes resembling the mullet and sole of Spain, heard what they thought to be nightingales, and saw trees and bushes resembling those at home; notably *Eugenia uniflora*, which they took to be myrtle. And as the champaign country at the head of the bay also recalled Castile, the Admiral "gave the name to the said island la Ysla Española" — the Spanish Isle. Peter Martyr latinized it as Hispaniola, which it still is.

Puerto de la Concepción, when Samuel de Champlain visited and mapped it in 1599, had become Port aux Mousquittes, owing to a particularly vicious anopheles of the neighborhood which raised painful blisters on sleeping sailors. Columbus's men, however, were too busy with pretty Indian girls to bother about mosquitoes. For it was here that they first made friendly contact

with the Arawaks of Haiti. A young and beautiful girl, clad only in a little V-shaped thing of cotton and a gold nose-plug, was captured and brought on board the flagship. "The Admiral had her clothed and gave her glass beads and hawk's bells and brass rings, and he sent her ashore very honorably, according to his custom." This good usage made it possible for the Spaniards to visit a big native village in the interior, where they were regaled with roast sweet potatoes. They reported that the Indians here were lighter in color and fairer of face than those of Cuba. But — no gold other than the girl's nose-plug, which she was allowed to keep. It is reported that she liked the Spaniards so much that she wished to sail away with them; but Columbus declined. He thought it might make trouble with the local Indians, and it would certainly have complicated relations with the crew of *Santa María.*

Departing 14 December, the two ships made little progress in Tortuga Channel against east wind and current, and the following night anchored in a cove near the mouth of the river now called Trois Rivières, owing to its three mouths (v.7). Columbus named it El Río Guadalquivir after the river of Seville, and the valley, Del Paraiso. He had himself rowed upstream to a spot where in April 1939 we found *haitiennes* both old and young washing themselves and their clothes. Colonel Cham of the Garde d'Haiti gravely introduced Morison to an old lady dressed only in a breechclout; she, in excellent

v.7

French and with perfect dignity, indicated the path to the river mouth, capping our thanks with, "*Il n'y a pas de quoi, mon Colonel; à votre service, M. le Professeur.*"

Next day the ships made but a few miles to windward and anchored off a big Indian village, probably on the site of Port-de-Paix. Shortly after Columbus anchored, about five hundred Indians appeared on the beach with their chief, a youth of some twenty-one years, supported by a council of elders. The Indians wore in their ears and noses grains of the finest gold, which they freely offered to the Spaniards. The Admiral wrote, "They are the best people in the world, and the gentlest; and above all I hope in Our Lord that Your Highnesses will make them all Christians, and that they will be all your subjects, for as such I hold them." Yet, in his Journal of the same day, addressing the Queen, Columbus suggests the slavery that was destined to exterminate these gentle natives: "They . . . are completely defenseless and of no skill in arms, and very cowardly . . . so they are fit to be ordered about and made to work, to sow and do all else that may be needed; and you may build towns and teach them to go clothed, and to [adopt] our customs."

On 18 December, the feast of Our Lady's Expectation, *Santa María* and *Niña* dressed ship and fired salutes. At noon, when the Admiral was dining in his cabin, the young chief came on board with his suite, ate a European meal with apparent relish, and received some simple gifts in return for valuable artifacts, such as a gold mask with precious stones inlaid. These — in fact all gold objects brought home by Columbus — were melted down in Spain.

v.8

Columbus took off next day after raising a cross in the village. After clearing Tortuga Channel, the ships had a fair wind along the coast, passing Marigot Island and Head (v.8); and Pointe Limbé, which the Admiral named Cabo Alto y Baxo (v.9). They then entered Acul Bay, which Columbus named La Mar de Sancto Thomé, since it was the vigil of the feast of St. Thomas the Apostle. The channel passes close aboard the little island which the Admiral appropriately named La Amiga but is now known as Rat Island (v.10).

Here Columbus found himself a veritable Venusberg. The modern name Acul is a rough approximation to the Spanish Ancon de Luisa, named after a

lady who kept an establishment there for the entertainment of sailors. She was hardly needed in Columbus's day, as the pretty native girls went completely naked, not even wearing the "little cotton things . . . like the flap of a man's drawers," which were *de rigueur* to the westward. They were in no way inhibited, and their menfolk were not jealous. And the scenery is magnificent. The mountains on either side compose like a landscape of Claude Lorraine, and on clear days one can see in the far distance the citadel of King Henri of Haiti, built in the early nineteenth century. Columbus wrote in his journal, "I have followed the sea for twenty-three years . . . and I have seen all the East and West and I have been to Guinea, but in all those regions will not be found the perfection of these harbors . . . so protected that one could moor with the ship's most ancient cable." That she could have done; Lombardo Cove, the inner harbor of Acul Bay, is so protected from all winds that a yacht once rode out a heavy norther there without tautening her anchor chain. The *Sailing Directions for the West Indies* calls it a "natural dock."

V.11

Besides giving themselves, the girls offered country products such as cassava bread, "nut-colored" shriveled "quinces" (*gonca avellanada*), which were either the sapodilla (v.11) or the custard apple (v.12), and five or six other kinds of fruit. Columbus later heard that the medicinal rhubarb grew there and sent a boat to gather a basketful; but, alas, it turned out to be what the French call roioc or *fausse rhubarbe*. How pathetic it is that Columbus loaded his vessels' holds with all manner of worthless plants such as agave, gumbo-limbo, false cinnamon, nuts that weren't coconuts, and this rhubarb — while ignoring others like maize, cassava, tobacco and rubber that have spread world-wide! He did, however, value the several species of wild cotton (v.13), because cotton in Spain was then a luxurious imported fiber.

V.13

This paradise is almost deserted today except for Negro fishermen who are so poor that they ply their calling from bamboo rafts with homemade reed sails like the one we saw in 1939 (v.14).

The Spaniards tarried in Acul Bay long enough to send a boat ahead to the seat of the cacique of that region, Guacanagarí, at Fort Liberté Bay, and to bring back an invitation to call. The messenger brought, as earnest of the cacique's good intentions, a remarkable belt of white and colored fishbones sewed in a pattern like embroidery, and to which was attached a mask with ears, tongue and nose of solid gold. After receiving such convincing evidence of wealth, the Admiral wasted no more time at Acul Bay. On their last night in this enchanting place, the men entertained on board an estimated one thousand Indians who came in dugouts, in addition to half as many more who swam out.

Early on 24 December the two ships departed with the land breeze, rounded Pointe Picolet (v.15), the outstanding promontory of Cap Haitien (which Columbus named Cabo Santo because it was Christmas Eve), and by nightfall were well across Cape Haitien Bay. There then occurred the most serious accident of any of Columbus's four voyages.

The wind fell away to light airs from the west, the men were exhausted from their efforts and pleasures of the previous night, and everyone in the flagship except a small boy at the helm fell asleep. At a few minutes before midnight there was a crash, as the ground swell dropped *Santa María* on a reef. The shock brought everyone on deck. Columbus ordered the master, Juan de la Cosa, to take the ship's boat and run out an anchor astern so she could be kedged off; but La Cosa, emulating some of St. Paul's shipmates (Acts 27:30), took this as an opportunity to desert the Admiral and flee to *Niña*, which had avoided the reef. Her captain, Vicente Yañez Pinzón, loyally refused to receive the deserters, and by the time they returned to the flagship it was too late to save her. The ground swell and rising tide had

v.15

v.16

pushed her so hard onto the reef that she could not be got off, even by cutting away her masts and jettisoning the guns and ballast.

This fatal reef lies about halfway between the Limonade Pass in the barrier reef, which our air photograph (v.16) shows, and the cluster of white houses at the right, which is the Haitian village of Limonade Bord-de-Mer. The reef itself is here, with a big curler breaking over it (v.17). Cacique Guacanagarí and his subjects turned out to help, but nothing could be done to save *Santa María*. Columbus then decided to make the best of a bad situation, build a fort ashore, leave a garrison therein, and return home in *Niña*.

v.17

This was done. The fort was constructed out of the flagship's planks and timbers hard by a roadstead where the local fishing fleet anchors today, and where the French built a fort in colonial days (v.18). Columbus named it La Villa de Navidad because the accident happened early Christmas morning, and the anchorage Puerto de la Navidad. He had no trouble in obtaining volunteers to remain, because their mission was to discover the gold mine whence, the cacique assured them, the metal of his gold ornaments was derived. The fort was abundantly stocked with provisions and trading truck salvaged from *Santa María*. Diego de Harana, marshal of the fleet and brother to the Admiral's Cordovan mistress, was placed in command, and 38 others volunteered to remain. All was completed by New Year's Day 1493.

v.18

After a state visit to Guacanagarí, whose seat was on the modern Fort Liberté Bay a few miles to the eastward (v.19), *Niña* sailed out through the pass in the barrier reef on 4 January 1493, and resumed exploration of the northern coast.

The site of Navidad was well chosen, but the garrison was not. Here, in November 1493, on his Second Voyage Columbus experienced one of the most severe shocks in all his career. His flagship *Mariagalante*, leading a fleet of 16 other vessels, had romped before the trades from Samaná Bay in only

two days. The Admiral confidently expected to greet the garrison he had left in January, to hear where the gold mines were, and to debark hundreds of prospective settlers with horses, cattle, seed and plants, so that Villa de Navidad would become a proper colony. Arriving at nightfall off the great bay, unwilling to risk threading the reefs in darkness, the Admiral fired a gun as signal for the fleet to anchor. One after one they rounded into the dying breeze, dropped hooks, furled sails, and gazed anxiously toward Navidad, which lay only three miles to the southward. But no sign of life was there, no answering salute when the fleet's cannon was fired, no light responded to flares made in the iron cresset on the flagship's poop. Then, wrote one of Columbus's shipmates, "Sadness and the most poignant grief overcame them all, for they suspected what really had happened, that the comrades whom they had left there were all dead."

At 10 P.M. a canoe full of Indians approached from the shore, the paddlers calling, "Almirante! Almirante!" The captain of this party, a cousin of Guacanagarí, bore his greetings to the Admiral with a present of two golden masks. Wishing to please, he assured Columbus that the Christians were all right; but Diego the interpreter got the truth out of the Indians and conveyed it to his master. Columbus would not at first believe it. Surely some of the garrison must be alive? These timid, defenseless Indians could not have wiped out forty seamen, soldiers and gentlemen of Spain?

That, it turned out, is exactly what they had done. The Navidad garrison had not long been left to its own devices when the men began to quarrel over women and gold. A gang roving the island in search of more loot encountered a stout cacique, Caonabó, who put them to death, collected a force of warriors, and descended on Navidad to wipe out the source of trouble. In the meantime most of the other Christians had split up into rival gangs, living in huts apart — with five women apiece — and no proper guard at the fort. Caonabó was able to exterminate them piecemeal. No vestiges of Navidad were left except charred timbers and old clouts lying about. Guacanagarí pretended to have been wounded defending the Spaniards from Caonabó, but when Dr. Chanca, the fleet physician, undid his bandage, there was nothing. Columbus, however, concluded that the cacique was not guilty, and he remained a faithful ally to the Spaniards.

The Admiral made a quick decision to pitch no settlement here; and that was a mistake, as Le Cap, or Cap Haitien, which the French founded on that very bay in the seventeenth century, became "the Paris of the Antilles."

We may now resume our survey of the north coast of Hispaniola.

Niña, sailing eastward from Navidad in January and returning in November 1493, passed through a group of islands now called The Seven Brothers, and in the distance (as in our air photograph v.20) saw what appeared to be an island shaped like an *alfaneque,* a Moorish pavilion. Columbus named it

V.20

Monte Christo, and Monte Cristi is the name today of the nearby town. The hill is now called El Morro, and the peninsula La Granja — The Barn. We are now in the Dominican Republic, so the nomenclature is Spanish.

Three days (6-8 January 1493), when *Niña* lay windbound at a good anchorage between Monte Christi and Isla Cabrón (Buck Island), were employed in taking on wood and water and exploring the lower course of a nearby river. This, which Columbus called Río del Oro, is now the Yaque del Norte; its mouth is here shown, with Monte Cristi Bay where Columbus anchored between it and La Granja (v.21). Columbus reported this river to be so full of gold that grains of it adhered to the barrel hoops when they scraped the gravel while being filled with river water. Las Casas snorted over the story, but there is gold in that river today; a former planter told Morison that the country women pan it out patiently, and many by Christmastide will have collected a turkey-quill half full of gold dust, which they

V.21

can sell to advantage. In this river Columbus found his first virgin gold in the New World, and what he then collected was but a token of the wealth of the Cibao, which this river drained.

It was also at the Monte Cristi anchorage that Martín Alonso Pinzón in *Pinta* rejoined the Admiral in *Niña*. One would give anything for a record of the conversation that then took place! But the two caravels continued in company, and on 9 January 1493 anchored in the lee of Punta Rucia, which Columbus named Punta Roja on account of its reddish cliffs (v.22).

We must now shift to the Second Voyage. On 2 January 1494, after miserably beating to windward for 25 days, Columbus reached a spot where he decided to pitch his colony, and named it Isabela. It was a very poor site, with no good harbor, and the Bajabonico river a mile distant, the only source of fresh water. But the long beat had exhausted the people, and the livestock on board were dying; so Columbus founded a city which he expected to last for all time.

V.22

At Isabela, on 6 January, the Feast of the Epiphany, the first mass in the New World was celebrated by Fray Buil, head chaplain on the Second Voyage; and hence, next day, Alonso de Hojeda began exploring the Cibao, the gold-bearing region in the interior. But everything else at Isabela went wrong. The several hundred colonists, both gentlemen volunteers and those on the royal payroll, loathed the idea of planting crops and building a city; they wished to rove about the interior and extort gold from the Indians. Unaccustomed to the climate and to native food, some 350 men fell sick, and the medicaments gave out. Columbus's brother Diego, whom he left in charge when he departed on his exploration of southern Cuba, proved to be a wretched administrator. Michele de Cuneo declared, "Although the soil is very black and good they have not yet found the way nor the time to sow; the reason is that nobody wants to live in these countries." So, when Columbus departed for Spain in March 1496, he and his brother Bartholomew decided to found a new capital city, and pitched on the site of Santo Domingo, which the Adelantado Bartholomew founded in the Admiral's absence. Isabela was abandoned, the ruins of the monumental city that the Columbus brothers had built disintegrated, and were reported to be haunted (v.23). In Washington Irving's day a few pillars of the church, and the ruins of a fort and of a stone house were still visible; fifty years later, the *Sailing Directions for the*

V.23

West Indies recorded, "The cupidity of the neighbouring inhabitants has not respected these venerable vestiges; the walls having been broken down, and the materials carried to Puerto Plata and other places to erect houses." Early in the twentieth century the site had become a mere pasture by the sea.

The rest of the north coast of Hispaniola, stretching about 125 miles from Isabela to Cape Samaná, was ranged by Columbus at least thrice: eastward in January 1493 in *Niña*, when it took just a week; westward in November 1493 in *Mariagalante*, in two days; eastward again in *Niña*, in March 1496, when she required ten days.

On his First Voyage, sailing from Monte Cristi in company with *Pinta* on 9 January 1493, Columbus rounded Cape Isabela and anchored within Puerto Blanco. Martín Alonso in *Pinta* had already been there, trading with the natives for gold, and had named the harbor after himself; the Admiral would have none of that and renamed it Río de Gracia, probably because he had forgiven his runaway captain. But, he adds with a bit of malice, in that harbor were *mucha broma* (many teredos), which enjoyed boring into *Pinta*'s planking while Martín Alonso was making money, and made her leak badly. Puerto Blanco is a pretty, protected harbor with two arms (v.24), and the shores are now well cultivated.

V.24

A few miles east of it, on 11 January 1493, Columbus sighted a mountain that he named Monte de Plata because the summit was covered by a silver cloud. The neat little harbor tucked in under its northwestern slope is still called Puerto Plata (v.25), although the mountain's name has been changed to Loma Isabela de Torres. Christopher and Bartholomew Columbus inspected the place on the former's return passage in *Niña* in 1496, with a view to establishing a new capital there to replace Isabela. But they decided in favor of the Río Ozama, across the island. Bartolomé de las Casas, who later became prior of a Dominican monastery on the slope of Monte Plata, is amusingly indignant over the rejection of his home port. Santo Domingo, he says, was selected because Miguel Díaz, who reconnoitered the site, fell in love with Catalina, the lady cacique of that part of Hispaniola, and wanted to be near her! However that may be, Santo Domingo was the right choice; Puerto Plata is small and open to northers.

v.25

From Puerto Plata, *Niña* in 1493 passed Cabo Macoris, which Columbus named Cabo del Angel, and another high cape which he called Cabo Francés, "on the east side of which is a great bay; but it didn't seem to have an anchorage." True enough, as that bay is exposed to the easterly trades. The cape is now called Cabo Viejo Francés so as not to be confused with Cap Haitien, which in the colonial era was called Cap Français. Sailing on a bowline across Bahía Escocesa, *Niña* rounded the modern Cabo Cabrón, which the Admiral named Cabo Padre y Hijo (Father and Son), on account of its two cliffy promontories (v.26). He then steered southeast to a cape "beautiful and high and rotund, all of rock, like Cape St. Vincent in Portugal." This was Cape Samaná (v.27), which has sheer reddish-brown cliffs rising to a height of 500 feet, and closely resembles Cape St. Vincent. Columbus romantically named it Cabo del Enamorado, after some "lover's leap" he had seen in Spain.

Past Cape Samaná, there opened "a very great bay, three leagues broad, and in the midst of it an *isleta pequeñuela*," a tiny little island. The bay is now called Samaná; President U. S. Grant once tried to obtain it from the Dominican Republic for a United States naval station. Cayo Levantado is the tiny island.

[95]

v.27

On the right of our photograph (v.28), on the northern shore of the gulf facing the bay, will be observed a white sand beach. The point next it is still called Las Flechas (The Arrows), because Columbus here came as near as he ever did on his First Voyage to a fight with the natives. The local Arawaks, known as the Ciguayos, more exposed to Carib raids than their fellows to the westward, were not the gentle, defenseless people whom hitherto the Spaniards had met. Columbus described them as very ugly, with charcoal-stained faces and long coarse hair gathered behind in nets of parrot feathers; and they

v.28

had adopted the Carib arms. When *Niña*'s boat crew landed, they were received by some fifty of these Indians armed with bows and arrows and palm-tree cudgels. After a Spaniard had boldly closed the group and slashed one of them on the buttocks with his sword, *Niña*'s interpreter persuaded them to drop their weapons. This photograph (v.29), posed by Caribs in Dominica for the J. Arthur Rank film *Christopher Columbus*, gives one a fair idea of what Columbus's men encountered at Las Flechas, although the Ciguayos carried clubs instead of spears as auxiliary weapons.

v.29

Columbus took his departure in *Niña* from Samaná Bay on 16 January 1493, and returned in November, going ashore to bury a Spaniard who had been mortally wounded in the fight at St. Croix, and to return to his home a Ciguayo whom he had kidnapped.

The east and south coasts of Hispaniola were discovered on his Second, Third and Fourth Voyages. On 22 November 1493, sailing across the Mona

Passage from Añasco Bay, Puerto Rico, Columbus discovered Cape Engaño, the eastern promontory of Hispaniola, and named it Cabo San Rafaël, after the Archangel. He was astonished to find it so low and flat, in contrast to the mountainous capes he had passed on the First Voyage. Our photograph (v.30) shows this uninhabited cape with its salt lagoons as it appeared under an overcast on 25 May 1963.

On the same day we obtained, under similar difficulties, a photograph of the low, fertile and reef-rimmed Saona Island off the southeast point of Hispaniola (v.31), where Columbus in September 1494 rode out a near-hurricane in safety. This owes its name to the fact that "out of love for me," wrote Michele de Cuneo of Savona, "the Lord Admiral called it La Bella Saonese. He gave it to me as a present, and I took possession of it according to the appropriate modes and forms, as the Lord Admiral was doing of the other islands in the name of His Majesty the King; that is, by virtue of a document signed by a notary public. On the above-mentioned island I uprooted grass and cut trees and planted the cross and also the gallows, and in the name of God I baptized it with the name La Bella Saonese. And well it is called beautiful, for in it are 37 villages with at least 30,000 souls." A pretty picture indeed:— two old comrades from the Republic of Genoa creating a new Savona with old-world ceremonies. But Michele never returned to claim his island, or to hang anyone on the gallows.

A few miles west of Saona is the island Catalina, which according to Las Casas was named by Columbus after the lady cacique of Higuey. His fleet, calling there just before reaching Saona, found the natives threatening them with bows and poisoned arrows, and holding cords to bind any Christian who presumed to land. But when they recognized the Admiral, whose reputation for good usage had evidently got around, they dropped their weapons and provided water and provisions.

The next point of Columbian interest, and a great one indeed, is the city of Santo Domingo, which Bartholomew founded during his brother's absence in Spain, and Christopher first saw at the conclusion of his Third Voyage, in 1498. He left it two years later a town of palm-thatch, wood and wattle; but his son Don Diego Colón, Second Admiral and Viceroy of the Indies, rebuilt

V.31

Santo Domingo in stone, around a plaza and a great viceregal palace. This palace we show as it appeared in ruins in 1890 (v.32), and as it appears today after a thorough restoration by the late dictator Trujillo (v.33). We can,

however, show one thing which Christopher Columbus may have seen at Santo Domingo. That is the great ceiba or silk-cotton tree on the edge of the harbor, the Río Ozama, to which according to tradition Columbus used to secure a cable from his ship when foul weather threatened. It is certain that the tree was already big in 1500, and that it served hundreds of vessels as a sort of land anchor until it died, early in the present century. Our photo (v.34) was taken around 1880 by William Robertson Cabot of Boston, who also photographed the old water gate to the city, which dates from 1500 (v.35).

v.34

The Cathedral of Santo Domingo, metropolitan see in the New World, was begun in 1523 during the viceroyalty of Don Diego, and many times since enlarged and partly rebuilt. The recently restored sacristy, believed to be a part of the original edifice, we show under the reverent inspection of Obregón and Morison (v.36). Mortal remains of the great Discoverer are in the small casket shown under the marble monument erected to his memory inside the west portal of the Cathedral (v.37). The story of how they got there is long and complicated. Columbus was first buried at Valladolid, where he died in 1506. Three years later, his remains were reinterred at the monastery of Las Cuevas, Seville. Around 1541 his daughter-in-law the Vicereine Doña María de Colón y Toledo had the remains repacked in a small lead casket which, together with a similar casket containing those of her late husband Don Diego, was sent to Santo Domingo and buried there before the high altar of the Cathedral. Some 250 years later, when Spain ceded Hispaniola to Republican France, Columbus's official heir obtained permission to have his distinguished ancestor's remains removed to the Cathedral of Havana. But the workmen at Santo Domingo dug up the wrong casket, that of Don Diego; and it was this one which, after Cuba became independent, was removed to Seville, and around which a magnificent tomb has been constructed, as that of the Discoverer.

V.37

In the meantime, while the presbytery of the Santo Domingo Cathedral was being enlarged in 1877-78, the real Christopher Columbus casket was found, and both the inscription on the outside and that on the inside cover, which Rudolph Cronau saw and copied (v.38), leave no doubt that these are the veritable remains of the Discoverer. They are now enclosed in the monument which we photographed in 1963.

Ill^tre y E_s de Varon D^n. Criztoval Colon   v.38

Columbus lived for two years, very unhappily, at Santo Domingo. Spanish and Indian subjects were making all kinds of trouble. In October 1500, the royal inquisitor Bobadilla arrested him and his brothers and sent them, in chains, to Spain. Partially restored to royal favor, he returned in *La Capitana*, flagship of his Fourth Voyage, in June 1502. Ferdinand and Isabella had ordered him not to go ashore without permission of the new viceroy, Don Nicolás de Ovando, who not only refused to let the Admiral enter the harbor but mocked honest Pedro de Terreros whom he had sent to give warning that a hurricane was making up. As Columbus wrote to the Sovereigns, "What man ever born, not excepting Job, would not have died of despair, when in such weather, seeking safety for my son, my brother, shipmates and myself, we were forbidden access to the land and the harbors which I, by God's will and sweating blood, had won for Spain?"

His fleet, when the hurricane struck in, was anchored in the roadstead off the Río Negua mouth ten miles west of Santo Domingo (v.39). *Capitana*'s ground tackle held, the other three caravels were driven out to sea, but all four rendezvoused, somewhat battered, in a little landlocked harbor to the westward which Columbus named Puerto Escondido. It is now Puerto

Viejo de Azúa (v.40). In the meantime, a Spanish fleet of some 25 sail which the insolent Ovando had sent to sea, disregarding Columbus's warnings, encountered the full force of the hurricane in Mona Passage with Cape Engaño under their lee. Twenty ships were lost with all hands, three or four managed to work back into Santo Domingo, and of all this proud fleet only the smallest and meanest, which was carrying Columbus's own gold to Spain, got through. Divine justice, said the Admiral's friends; sorcery and witchcraft, hissed his enemies!

V.41

West of Azúa the Hispaniola coast is steep-to and mountainous; the turning point, where one alters course from southwest to northwest, is Alta Vela, a rock which does indeed look like a high sail (v.41). Columbus so named it on his return from Cuba in *Niña* in 1494. His men climbed to the summit to search the horizon for the other two caravels, which had been separated from the flagship in a gale. It took these six days to catch up; and in the meantime Columbus's men hunted seal and wild pigeon, and *Niña* harbored behind Beata Island (v.42), which Columbus named Madama Beata after the Blessed Virgin, whose nativity feast he passed there. Four years later, on his Third Voyage, he made landfall on Alta Vela and spent three days at anchor in the Beata Island harbor.

V.42

The next port westward associated with Columbus is Jacmel, Haiti (v.43), which the natives called Yaquino and the Admiral named Puerto Brazil, from the quantities of brazil or logwood found nearby, the commercial importance of which he recognized. Logwood is still essential to make a fast black, and is still being exported from Haiti. Our specimen of the wood and flowers of the most common West Indian logwood, *Peltophorum Linnaei*, was photographed by Crofoot in the garden of the College of Tropical Agriculture, Trinidad (v.44). Of similar provenance is his photograph of a magnificent

v.43

[107]

v.44

rubber tree, *Castilla elastica*, with its leaves exhibited by Priscilla Morison and Dr. John Purseglove (v.45). For, besides brazilwood and other Hispaniola flora, Cuneo mentions "trees which when cut give a milk of which they make

v.45

something like wax, and we have tried it out." Certain botanists deny that the rubber tree then grew as far north as Hispaniola, but Dr. Purseglove convinced us that *Castilla elastica* is what Cuneo describes. The Spaniards are not be be blamed for failing to recognize the commercial importance of the "something like wax," because no other Europeans did prior to the nineteenth century.

Ile Vache (v.46), the next landmark west, protects the large harbor of Aux Cayes, which Columbus passed thrice; and that takes us to the western

v.46

promontory of the ancient kingdom of Xaragua. Columbus called it Cabo San Miguel after merry Michael of Savona; but that name was later replaced by the more appropriate one of Cabo Tiburón, Cape Shark (v.47).

We have now covered the entire coast of Hispaniola that Columbus saw. He never entered the great Leogane Gulf, where Port-au-Prince was founded by the French in the eighteenth century.

v.47

CHAPTER VI

The Windward and
Leeward Islands

COLUMBUS visited none of the Lesser Antilles south of Martinique. On 14 August 1498, after sortieing from the Boca del Dragón, he took a hitch to the east and north, sighted from afar Tobago, which he named La Isla de la Asunción (since it was the vigil of the Assumption of the Virgin), and Grenada, which he called La Concepción. But he never touched at either island, or ever sighted the Grenadines, Barbados and St. Vincent. He must have seen St. Lucia when passing south of Martinique on his Fourth Voyage, and he certainly saw the curious Diamond Rock (vi.1).

vi.2

On that voyage his landfall was Martinique, and he made it on 15 June 1502, twenty-one days from the Grand Canary, his shortest ocean passage. After viewing the east coast (vi.2), and knowing by experience that he could find no harbor on the windward side, he rounded the southern end. Columbus's immediate object at the end of every long voyage was to find a protected anchorage with a river, where he could fill his water casks and his men could wash themselves and their clothes. The first harbor on the leeward coast of Martinique, Cul-de-Sac Marin (vi.3), had too many reefs at the entrance; so he continued a few miles farther and anchored in the Baie de Sainte Luce,

vi.3

where there was a river of sweet water and no obstructions (vi.4). As he was in a hurry to get on, he made no effort to explore Martinique. As soon as the water butts were filled and wood cut for the galley fire, he passed outside the harbor of Fort-de-France, one of the best in the Antilles. He had heard of Martinique from his Indian guides on the First Voyage, under a name that he rendered as Matinino; they told a tall tale to the effect that this island was inhabited only by women, who invited a party of men to visit them once a year for purposes of procreation, and then sent them packing. Columbus's ex-experiences with the natives of Guadeloupe in 1496 satisfied him that that was the Amazon Island, and he had seen more than enough of the ferocious females there. So, on this Fourth Voyage, he made best speed to Santo Domingo where, as we have seen in Chapter V, he was not allowed to land.

The next island north, Dominica, was the American landfall of his Second Voyage. A sharp lookout in flagship *Mariagalante* picked it up, 24 days out from Gomera, at dawn on Sunday, 3 November 1493; hence the name. The Admiral promptly "summoned all hands on deck, sang the *Salve Regina* and

vi.4

other hymns and prayers very devoutly, rendering thanks to Our Lord for so short and prosperous a passage." As daylight increased, they sighted Guadeloupe, Marie-Galante, The Saints, and probably Deseada, now Désirade.

Dominica, wrote Nicolo Syllacio in his tract on the Second Voyage, "is notable for the beauty of its mountains and the charm of its verdure. A thick growth of trees extends to the water's edge, as in the Vale of Tempe in Thessaly." As our close-up of a cove at the north end shows (vi.5), Dominica is one of the most beautiful islands of the Antilles, and the one least spoiled by twentieth-century "progress" and "development." Columbus, as yet ignorant of the ironbound windward coast of the Lesser Antilles, searched in vain for

vi.5

a harbor on the east side of the island, but sent a caravel around the northern point and into Prince Rupert's Bay (vi.6), the nearest thing to a harbor in Dominica.

Dominica was protected from European domination by tough, man-eating Caribs until the early eighteenth century, when it was conquered by France. From the name of this tribe the Caribbean, the Caribee Isles, and the word cannibal are derived. A favorite story of the colonial period told of a Spanish Franciscan captured and eaten by the Caribs, who fell so sick that never again would they eat a European dressed in sackcloth and with a shaved tonsure. Consequently, when a crew becalmed off Dominica badly needed wood or water, and if no Franciscan was on board, they shaved a sailor's head, dressed him in a gunny-sack with a rope around his middle, and sent him ashore to do business.

vi.6

The only reservation of Caribs, or of any Indians in the Lesser Antilles to-day, is in northeastern Dominica; a reservation approached by an atrocious road (vi.7) bordered by tree ferns (which apparently Columbus never noticed), and numbering barely 600 souls. Even so, the Negroes who have supplanted the old master class in Dominica are constantly encroaching on the

vi.8

vi.7

reservation and burning down sections of it to plant corn and bananas. The surviving Caribs preserve a distinctly American Indian cast of countenance, but dress like anyone else in the West Indies (vi.8), unless specially rigged for photographic purposes, which we had no time to do. They, and the Negroes too, build dugout canoes in the traditional manner, widening the hollowed hardwood log by filling it with stones and boiling water; the one which we observed (vi.9) had its topsides built up with boards and could be propelled by oar or sail as well as paddle.

vi.9

Returning to Columbus's Second Voyage: while the one caravel reconnoitered Dominica, Columbus and the rest of the fleet proceeded to a round, flat island which the Admiral named Mariagalante, the nickname of his gallant flagship. Marie-Galante, as it is still called, has no harbor, but the fleet anchored on the lee side, which is now intensively cultivated with sugarcane (vi.10). Here the Admiral went ashore and took possession of the entire region for Spain. His men observed the manzanilla or manchineel tree, whose leaves, they said, "dripped poison," but this was not correct. *Hippomane mancinella* does produce an apple-like fruit which poisoned many a Spaniard who tried eating it, and gave the manchineel a bad name; but the tree itself is sufficiently safe to be used as an ornamental plant in these islands today (vi.11).

vi.10

Before daylight 4 November the fleet weighed anchor from off Mariaga-
lante and steered toward a big, high island which had already been sighted.
En route they discovered a group of four small, rugged islands which Columbus named Todos los Santos after All Saints' Day just past (vi.12).
These are now Les Saintes, off which was fought the great naval Battle of The
Saints on 12 April 1782, in which Admiral Rodney broke the French line of
battle and captured Admiral de Grasse in his flagship *Villa de Paris*. Les
Saintes were settled by fisherfolk from Brittany whose descendants live there
today and build most of the small sailing craft used in the French Antilles.

The big, mountainous island which the Caribs called something like Kerkeria was renamed by Columbus Santa María de Guadalupe, after the Virgin of Guadalupe, the early medieval statue in the Convento de los Jerónimos in Estremadura. There the Admiral had stayed between voyages, and promised the monks to name an island after their Virgin (vi.13). No Spaniard ever succeeded in settling this big island, but the French under d'Esnambuc did so in 1635; and Guadeloupe, as they named it, now boasts of being the oldest French colony.

As Columbus's fleet approached this island, they saw its principal marvel: a waterfall that appeared to fall from clouds hanging low on the volcanic peak of La Soufrière. We are particularly proud to show this photograph of it, (vi.14), as well as the frontispiece, because nobody before caught both the upper and the lower falls, with the former appearing to drop right out of the clouds. The sight of it puzzled Columbus's men. Dr. Chanca wrote, "Many wagers were laid in the ships; some said it was white rocks and others that it was water."

vi.13

vi.14

Syllacio wrote, "Those who beheld this wonderful sight from the ships wondered at first whether it was the glistening of closepacked snow or the broad highway of an old road."

"It was the fairest thing in the world," concluded Dr. Chanca, "to see from what a height it fell and from how small a space so great a waterfall arose."

Guadeloupe, according to Syllacio, "held the seamen close in its spell, with its wide and beautiful plains and the indescribable beauty of its mountains." One is constantly struck in the writings of Columbus and his shipmates by their wonder at and appreciation of the beauties of nature; for similar reactions from discoverers are unusual prior to the eighteenth century. The plains of Guadeloupe are mostly in the eastern part, which the French call Grande-Terre, and which Columbus and his men saw from afar but did not visit.

[121]

These waterfalls of the Grand Carbet river were the magnet that drew Columbus's fleet to the southern shore of Basse-Terre, the westerly part of Guadeloupe. Owing to the east wind they did not beat up into Petit Cul-de-Sac Marin, where the good harbor of Pointe-à-Pitre is located, but scudded downwind along the steep-to shore until they reached a good anchorage in what is now known as La Grande Anse (vi.15).

Here Columbus first encountered Carib Indians, since, on this voyage, nobody landed at Dominica. The fleet tarried at Grande Anse six days because a shore party under Diego Marquez got lost in the heavy, dank forest, with trees so high and dense that they could not even make out the stars. Four search parties of fifty men each, provided with tumpets and lanterns, almost got lost too; but eventually all straggled back. In the meantime, the Spaniards left on board explored the shore and destroyed all the Carib canoes they found, in order to prevent these Indians from raiding and eating their Arawak friends.

vi.15

They admired the great hardwood trees and tasted their first pineapples, one of which is depicted for the first time in Oviedo's 1535 edition (vi.15). Peter Martyr describes this fruit as "scaly, like a pine cone in appearance but of a prettier shape, but soft like a melon, surpassing every garden fruit and flavor, for it is no tree but a weed, resembling the thistle or acanthus; the King too gives it the palm." Peter adds regretfully that he never tasted a pineapple himself because only one survived the ocean passage — and the King ate it!

The shore parties encountered no Carib warriors but gathered evidence of their bestial habits. Choice cuts of human flesh were found in abandoned huts, two caponized boys who were being fattened for a feast were rescued and taken on board, together with "twelve very beautiful and very fat girls from 15 to 16 years old," destined for the same fate. All these, Arawak captives, were so delighted to be rescued that when the Admiral proposed to set them ashore again, "They clung to the masts, holding fast with locked legs, and . . . implored us not to force them back into the hands of the Caribs, like sheep to the slaughter." Columbus put them to work, of course, and eventually sent them to Spain.

Despite their abominable taste for human flesh, the Caribs were greatly admired by the Spaniards. Syllacio writes, "Their houses were built of thick reeds interlaced in the form of canopies; we were moved to admiration by their elegance." (vi.17) All their woodworking was done with stone tools.

vi.16

vi.17

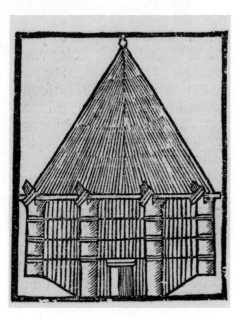

"The bow that they use in battle is exceptionally strong, and they shoot arrows the size of a walking stick, tipped with sharp bone barbs to keep the arrow from being easily withdrawn." Their cotton rugs were "so well woven that they owed nothing to those of our country." Carib artifacts are indeed more sophisticated than those of the simpler Arawaks. In our photograph (vi.18) Priscilla Morison is shown standing among the carved stones near Trois Rivières, which depict the creation myth of these Indians.

vi.18

Columbus once more landed on Guadeloupe in April 1496 on his return passage from the Second Voyage, in *Niña*, because he was already running short of bread and water. She and little *India*, built at Isabela, anchored in Grande Anse, where he had been three years earlier. Before their boats touched shore, a muster of Carib women rushed down to the beach and greeted the visitors with a shower of arrows. The Admiral then and there decided that Guadeloupe, not Martinique, was the Isle of Women he had heard about. Some Caribs earlier captured by the Spaniards, whom they were taking home to sell as slaves, were set ashore to tell their friends that the Christians wished them no harm, only wanted bread. The Amazons replied that they had none to spare, but their husbands, then in the northern part of the island, could supply what they wanted. So *Nina* and *India* sailed around the southwestern cape of the island until they came to a cove — probably Bouillante (vi.19)—

vi.19

where they found a large village. Again they were greeted with arrows, this time shot by men. But a few cannon shots sent them scampering into the jungle. An armed party pursued and captured three boys and ten women and, using these as hostages, managed to do business. The women sold them a quantity of cassava roots and taught them how to rasp them on a grater to make flour, and how to knead the flour into dough and bake it over the fire on a pottery griddle. Cassava bread has a pleasant flavor; it agreed with the Spaniards better than maize, and kept so well when properly baked that it became almost a staple ship provision.

vi.20

On 20 April 1496 *Niña* and *India* left this Guadeloupe anchorage for Spain,
taking along a lady cacique and her daughter at their own desire (so the Admiral asserted) as specimens of Amazons. Whether or not they survived the
voyage is not known, but the Admiral had some difficulty dissuading his men
from killing and eating them when food ran short; for, said they, the Caribs
eat people, so why should we not eat Caribs?

On 10 November 1493, the Second Voyage fleet outbound got under way,
destination Navidad; but they found plenty to interest them en route. Long
they lay becalmed under the lee of the Guadeloupe mountain range, and not
until noon next day did they reach "another island, not very big," about
thirty miles distant (vi.20). Columbus had already begun the pattern of naming islands after notable shrines of the Virgin. Guadeloupe honored the most
famous one in Castile, so this "not very big" but very beautiful island he called
Santa María de Monserrate, after the most famous shrine in Catalonia. Perhaps, too, its jagged skyline recalled that sharply serrated Catalan mountain
(vi.21). An ancient wooden statue of the Virgin and Child in the church of
the mountain monastery (vi.22) is greatly venerated.

vi.22

Columbus did not stop to investigate Montserrat, which has been called "The Emerald Island of the West." He noted a little round hump of an island, less than a mile long, which hardly rated a famous name, so called it Santa María la Redonda, St. Mary the Plump (vi.23). Redonda never has been inhabited, but in the last century a crazy Irishman bought it and declared his son to be Felipe I, King of Redonda, and Felipe was succeeded in 1947 by Juan I. Neither monarch ever set foot in his realm; both lived in England and amused themselves by creating their friends dukes and counts.

vi.22

Columbus himself may have seen Antigua from a distance. Assuming that he ordered some of his smaller caravels to fan out in a wide arc so as to miss nothing (as he had done when crossing Crooked Island Passage on the First Voyage), one of them probably reconnoitered that island (vi.24). The Admiral named it Santa María la Antigua after a medieval fresco of the Virgin

vi.24

and Child in the Cathedral of Seville (vi.25). That night he anchored his flagship and as many of the fleet as were within hailing distance, in the lee of an island that he named Nuestra Señora de las Nieves, Our Lady of the Snows. This name, following his system, was that of a famous Roman church dedicated to the Virgin. According to a charming legend depicted in Jorge Afonso's painting at Lisbon (vi.26), the Virgin appeared in their sleep to a

vi.25

pious Roman couple who had prayed for divine guidance as to the site of a
church they wished to found, and told them to locate it where snow fell. Next
day, 5 August, snow miraculously did fall on the Esquiline (observe the
Pope testing it with a shovel), and there they built the basilica, second oldest church in Rome; it used to be commonly called Santa Maria della Neve,
but is now best known as Santa Maria Maggiore. Every 5 August in the

commemoration mass little wisps of cotton wool are set adrift to recall the miracle. Our photograph shows the present Nevis near the spot where the Columbus fleet must have anchored, with St. Kitts beyond (vi.27).

Although there is no uncertainty about Columbus's course along the Lee-ward Islands, the nomenclature is confused. His shipmates who wrote about the voyage were not interested in jotting down details of small islands; and Juan de la Cosa, who drew a chart of them, was careless about names. On La Cosa's *mappemonde*, dated 1500, the island in the position of Nevis is named "*S. martin*," and "*S. de laniebe*" is placed on the second island beyond it. The name St. Martin makes sense because 11 November, the night that Columbus anchored off this island, is the feast of St. Martin of Tours. But there is another island of the outer fringe, some 60 miles north-northwest of Nevis, that has been called St. Martin for at least four centuries. Perhaps one of the small caravels discovered it next day; but, if so, she must also have seen St. Barthélemy and Anguilla, which are not mentioned, or recorded on La Cosa's chart. Nor, for that matter, did La Cosa put down Antigua.

vi.27

Columbus next discovered St. Christopher (commonly called St. Kitts), St. Eustatius (commonly called Statia), and Saba. St. Kitts is a curiously shaped island, with a ragged south end (vi.28) concealing a big salt lagoon, a mountainous middle and a narrow coastal plain so fertile that English and French sugar planters found it profitable to divide the island between them. In the eighteenth century Britain acquired the entire island, and several important naval battles between the royal navies of Britain and France were fought in these waters.

Columbus may have called this island after his patron saint; but, unlike most discoverers, he was reluctant to name places after himself and his family; and one of the early historians says that he called it St. George, after the patron saint of Genoa. A local tradition insists that the island was called St. Christopher because of a fancied resemblance of 3600-foot Middle Range and 4400-foot Mount Misery to the Saint carrying the Christ Child on his back. We could not see the resemblance, from either yacht or airplane; but the extinct

volcano on the next island, St. Eustatius (vi.29), might, with considerable imagination, be thought to confirm that legend. St. Eustatius, according to the *Isolario* of Alonso de Santa Cruz (1541) is a corruption of St. Anastasia, a virgin martyr whom Columbus may have had some reason to commemorate. But in our opinion St. Eustatius was the original St. Christopher, and the present St. Kitts was first called St. George. All these islands are close together, and so easily confused.

Saba, last of this chain, only two miles in diameter, rises to a height of 2900 feet. It has retained its Carib name. In the seventeenth century Saba was colonized by the Dutch, who still hold it, together with Statia (St. Eustatius) and half St. Martin. We encountered Saba under a heavy overcast, but the sun came out in time to show the steep northern shore of this tiny island which supports a thrifty population of several hundred souls, and where the Netherlands government has managed to hew out an airstrip (vi.30).

Somewhere in the lee of these last three islands the fleet hove-to for the night; Columbus, after the mishap of his First Voyage, never risked night sailing in unknown waters near shore. And what a sight that fleet hove-to must have been! Seventeen high-pooped vessels with riding sails catching the moonlight, masts describing circles against the starry dome, flares in the cressets reflected in the water. We may also envy the daytime delights of those Spanish sailors, even recapture them by ranging the Leeward Islands under sail. When sunrise kindles the high mountain peaks, the lower slopes shade from gray to green and then to a blue that blends with the sapphire sea. As the sun rises higher, the tradewind makes up and fat clouds begin to form on the windward side of the island you are approaching. At noon, under the land's lee, the wind dies and the ocean becomes a trembling mirror over which flying fish play. Afternoon brings a series of showers and black squalls that peter out quickly; and the massed clouds on mountain summits turn orange with the declining sun. Sometimes in winter the western horizon is so clear that the sun sends up a bright emerald flash from its spectrum as it dips under.

vi.30

vi.31

On the morning of 14 November 1493 Columbus sighted the island called by the Indians Ayay, by the Admiral Santa Cruz, and by us St. Croix. Passing the east point of the island (vi.31), the fleet sailed along the northern coast; the sailors rejoicing to see an island under cultivation, and anticipating a good time ashore, which they had not once enjoyed on this voyage. Since the reefs that protect the modern Christiansted Harbor were boiling in the surf, Columbus did not try to enter but brought his fleet to anchor outside the little harbor now known as Salt River Bay. Here is what he saw (vi.32), barring the modern houses and the white fresh-water catchments.

vi.32

Off Salt River Bay on that day occurred the first real fight between Christians and American pagans. The Admiral, wishing to speak with the inhabitants of a village inside the bay, and to get fresh water, sent an armed boat into the harbor. As the men landed, the natives fled. The boat's party then marched inland and captured a few of the Caribs' young Arawak slaves. As the boat was about to return to the flagship, a canoe paddled by four Carib men, two women and a boy came down the coast and halted, stupefied at the sight of strange vessels. When the Spaniards in the boat tried to get between canoe and shore, the Caribs "with great courage took up their bows, women as well as men," recorded Dr. Chanca, and wounded two of the boat's crew of over 25, one mortally. The boat then rammed and sank the canoe, but the Caribs swam to a rock awash — probably one of those shown breaking at the top of our photograph (vi.33), shooting even from the water and fighting ferociously until they were overcome and taken. One of these prisoners, who had been shot up until his intestines hung out, was pronounced by Dr. Chanca to be so far gone that the seamen threw him overboard; but he managed to

vi.33

swim, holding onto his guts with one hand. The Spaniards pursued and pulled him out, bound him hand and foot, and again tossed him into the sea. Even so, he managed to shuffle off his bonds and swim; so this "resolute barbarian" was shot through and through until he perished.

This had no sooner happened when great numbers of horribly painted Caribs came running down to the point of the harbor, shouting defiance and shooting arrows, which fell short of the ships. At the same time, numbers of Arawak captives swam out to them, seeking asylum.

The Spaniards were deeply impressed by the Caribs' stout courage; these were obviously natives to be respected and feared. And they were both amused and amazed by the conduct of "a very beautiful Carib girl" whom Michele de Cuneo had captured in the fight, and whom the Admiral presented to him as his slave. "Having taken her into my cabin," wrote Cuneo, "she being naked . . . I conceived a desire to take pleasure . . . but she did not want it and treated me with her finger nails in such fashion that I wished I had never begun! But, seeing that (to tell you the end of it), I took a rope and thrashed her well, for which she raised such unheard-of screams that you would not have believed your ears. Finally we came to an agreement in such a manner that I can tell you that she seemed to have been brought up in a school of harlots."

Columbus did not give this harbor a name, but he called the point where the Indians put up such a fight Cabo de la Flecha, Cape of the Arrow. He never set foot on St. Croix, but must have seen its rolling green contour once more on his Fourth Voyage, in 1502. It was perhaps owing to his shipmates' account of its cultivated fertility that Spain made considerable effort to colonize this island, and partly succeeded, by confining the Caribs to the less fertile part. Intruding French in the early seventeenth century gradually took over the whole island and renamed it Sainte-Croix. France sold it to Denmark in 1753; and Denmark sold it, together with her part of the Virgin Islands, to the United States in 1917. So we may say that St. Croix was the first bit of future United States soil that Columbus discovered. And it certainly provided his men with the first of a long series of battles that ended only when Geronimo the Apache, in North America, and the Araucanians of Chile, were subdued in the nineteenth century.

CHAPTER VII

The Virgin Islands and
Puerto Rico

AFTER DEPARTING from the roadstead off Salt River Bay, St. Croix, on the evening of 14 November 1493, Columbus's Second Voyage fleet ran into foul weather and hove-to, drifting eastward during the night, and possibly longer. On a clearing morning an intriguing archipelago was sighted to the northward. The nearer they came to it, the more islands appeared; so Columbus had the happy thought to name it after St. Ursula and the Eleven Thousand Virgins of Cologne.

According to this pleasant legend, St. Ursula, daughter of a king of Cornwall (maybe of King Mark of the Tristan and Isolde story), was promised in marriage to a pagan king of Brittany; but she, wishing to remain a Christian virgin, prevailed on the old man to give her a three-year cruise with her friends before coming to a firm decision. So many girl friends signed up that by the time the complement was complete there were no fewer than eleven thousand. The king, true to his word, provided his daughter with eleven vessels of the royal navy to conduct the cruise; one wonders how the seamen managed an average of a thousand girls per ship. The virgin fleet visited Rome and called on the Pope, who was so attracted by the prospect of cruising with eleven thousand pious girls that he abdicated the papal chair and came along, together with a bishop, the future St. Cyriacus. Details are wanting until, after some three years at sea, they were off the chops of the English Channel when a westerly gale made up and blew them right through to the mouths of the Rhine. Ursula then decided to sail up that river to visit the famous city of Cologne. It happened to be a bad moment; Attila and the Huns were attacking the city, and all hands were slaughtered. Princess Ursula

vii.1

was honored with sainthood, and her eleven thousand shipmates as martyrs.

A painting by Gregório Lopes (vii.1) in the Museu de Arte Antigua at Lisbon illustrates both the merry beginning and the tragic end to this feminine odyssey. In the background is shown the fleet of carracks, ships, and caravels, all contemporary to the artist and to Columbus. At the left, Ursula and two virgins embark and their parents, accompanied by local ecclesiastics, are giving them a reluctant bon voyage. In the center Ursula, several virgins, the ex-pope and Bishop Cyriacus are being set ashore at Cologne; and on the right they are being slaughtered by brutal and licentious soldiers dressed as fifteenth-century Turks. The Eleven Thousand Virgins became objects of veneration, not only at Cologne, but by sailors everywhere; there is an archipelago named after them — now called Burges — off Newfoundland, and Magellan named Cape Virgin, at the entrance of the strait that bears his name, Cabo de las Once Mil Vírgenes because he discovered it on their feast day, 21 October 1520. In no place, of course, were there so many islands; although in our case, if we counted every outlying rock and reef, we might run the score up to one thousand.

At daybreak 17 November the Columbian fleet hove-to off a big island, easternmost of the Virgins, which Columbus named St. Ursula, and some later and less reverent Spaniard called Virgen Gorda, the Pregnant Virgin (vii.2); it is still Virgin Gorda. Here the Admiral decided to divide his fleet.

[140]

While flagship *Mariagalante* and the big vessels jogged along south of the islands "clear in the main sea for fear of reefs," the caravels and small Cantabrian barques which Columbus had brought along for exploration fetched through the outer islands into what became known as Francis Drake Channel, after that great Englishman had sailed through it on his last voyage. We in Six-zero-Papa elected to follow the little vessels, passing the bluff on Beef Island (vii.3) on the starboard hand.

vii.3

The Virgin Islands have changed little in appearance since Columbus's day. They are largely uninhabited; and, as Peter Martyr wrote, they marvelously differ from one another, their rocks showing fantastic coloring — purple from the stone locally known as blue bit, dazzling white from Aeolian lime-stone or marl, which looked like marble to Columbus's fleet; while others are muffled in trees and herbage and bordered by pink coral beaches.

Now the small ships were looking straight down the Francis Drake Channel toward St. John (vii.4), probably so named by Columbus because the feast of St. John Chrysostom had just passed. Leaving Tortola on the starboard and St. John on the port hand, they threaded the Narrows and sailed through Pillsbury Sound, leaving the brightly colored Cabrita Point of St. Thomas on the starboard hand (vii.5), to join the big ships which were waiting for them somewhere in the lee of St. Thomas.

vii.4

Six-zero-Papa took a short cut across St. Thomas, whence Mr. Crofoot took this backward view (vii.6) of St. John and the Drake Channel.

Somewhere off the brisk modern port of Charlotte Amalie, St. Thomas, Columbus's great fleet made rendezvous at nightfall 17 November 1493.

On the 18th, some 20 miles west of St. Thomas, they picked up an island so fair with green verdure that Columbus named it Gratiosa after the mother of his friend Alessandro Geraldini, one of the ecclesiastics who had supported him in launching his great enterprise. Before he sailed, the Admiral had promised to bestow the name of Geraldini's mother, "famous for her high birth, holiness and old-fashioned manners," on "some noble island"; and here was the fulfilment. When Geraldini came out to the West Indies some nineteen years later as Bishop of Santo Domingo, he made a point of spending two days on Gratiosa, during which time he wrote, "The dear bosom of my mother . . . her adored and boundless caresses, and her joyful countenance as I recalled it from boyhood, never left me." Unfortunately, the name Gratiosa, recording filial piety and fraternal friendship, has been replaced by the native name Vieques — Crab (vii.7). But the beauty remains; a large part of the island, as we saw it, is green pasture.

Having sighted a great mountainous island some ten miles west of Gratiosa, Columbus hove his fleet to on the night of 18-19 November, in order safely to examine the big island next day. This was the one which the native Arawaks called Borinquen, and the Admiral named San Juan Bautista; for the relics of St. John the Baptist were held in great veneration at Genoa. One of his shipmates, Juan Ponce de León, marked this island for himself, entered and conquered it in 1506, and founded the city of San Juan on an excellent

vii.7

harbor on the northern coast. That city, to distinguish it from others of the same name, became known as San Juan de Puerto Rico, St. John of the Rich Harbor; and Puerto Rico eventually replaced San Juan Bautista as the name of the entire island.

All day 19 November the grand fleet ranged the southern, reef-fringed coast of Puerto Rico; a run of about a hundred miles in the thirteen or so hours of daylight, an average of about eight knots. Our view (vii.8), taken near Aguirre, gives a good sample of the barrier reef, the rich coastal plain and the sierra. That night they anchored under the lee of Cape Rojo, probably so named by Columbus on account of its red cliffs (vii.9).

Next morning they stood around Punta Aguila, hauled in their sheets and sailed northerly on a taut bowline in search of a good harbor to obtain wood and water. For, owing to the fight at St. Croix, they had been unable to replenish since Guadeloupe; and a good shipmaster like Columbus never missed an opportunity to fill his water butts and cut wood for the galley fires.

The question of what bay or harbor on the west side they put into on 20 November is a matter of sharp if friendly discussion among Puerto Rican historians. Boquerón Bay, the first bay on that side, visible in our photograph of Cape Rojo, has its partisans; so have Combate Beach near Cape Rojo, Mayagüez Harbor, and Aguadilla Bay. After examining the terrain and reading the works of Drs. Adolfo de Hostos and Aurelio Tió, we decided that the only seamanlike course for Columbus to have taken from Cape Rojo would have led him to Añasco Bay (vii.10). The argument for Añasco is clinched by the fact that Ponce de León, who was with Columbus in 1493, landed there thirteen years later, founded his first settlement nearby, and thence departed in 1511 on his voyage in search of the Fountain of Youth. The mouth of the Añasco river (vii.11) is doubtless the spot where the Spanish first landed.

vii.10

As proof of the interest in this question in Puerto Rico, Dr. Tió printed
Morison's letter backing him up on Añasco; whereupon Mr. Carmelo Filardi
published in *El Mundo* of San Juan this amusing cartoon *¿Por donde llego
Colón?* of "Juan del Pueblo," the John Citizen of Puerto Rico, sitting on the
highest mountain of the island and reading the letter (vii.12), which says,
" 'Elio Tió is right, Añasco it was," and he remarks, "Still better, I put in for
Jayuya!" which is the name of the mountain.

Columbus spent but two nights in this Puerto Rican bay, and never returned. Information as to what happened there comes from number of people who picked up their information after the fleet returned to Spain. One
says that the sailors who wandered inland found "a very big and fair house
abandoned; they estimated that in a certain season some important person
came there to live for his pleasure." This mansion was surrounded, as in a
plaza, by twelve small houses, also abandoned. The great house was roofed
with verdure "like the garden arbors of Valencia," and that place was connected by road with the bay, on the edge of which was a high watch
tower. The site of this important village has not yet been established by

vii.12

archaeologists; but it was no winter resort. The Arawaks of Puerto Rico lived in constant terror of Carib raids; and, having no canoes in which to escape, took to the mountains as soon as they saw strange craft approaching by sea. Columbus never met a single native of Puerto Rico.

[148]

After taking on wood and water, the fleet departed Añasco Bay at day-break 22 November, and steered toward Hispaniola on a course suggested by the Arawak guides. En route and from a distance they picked up the flat island of Mona (vii.13), which gives its name to this passage between Puerto Rico and Hispaniola. Peter Martyr, the classicist, supposed that Columbus called it after the Latin name for Angelsea; but it is more likely derived from *amona*, one of the native names for cassava, of which it was a veritable wild garden in the colonial era.

On 23 November the fleet made a cape which the Indians said was Hispaniola. Columbus at first insisted that it could not possibly be Hispaniola because it was flat as a pancake and no mountains were visible. The Indians, however, were right. This was Cape Engaño, for a photograph of which see illustration v. 30 (page 98). We have already described in Chapter V his course from that cape of Hispaniola.

vii.13

CHAPTER VIII

Trinidad and Paria

ON HIS Third Voyage of June through August 1498, Columbus deliberately chose a more southerly transatlantic route than on the first two, hoping to find a continental land mass, sophisticated Orientals, and more abundant gold than he had hitherto discovered. In a flagship of about one hundred tons named *Santa María de Guía*, and two small caravels *Vaqueño* and *Correo*, he began the ocean crossing on 4 July from São Tiago in the Cape Verde Islands. Soon they ran into the doldrums, where the fleet was becalmed and the people suffered agonies from the heat, since Europeans in those days would never strip off their heavy woolen clothes and risk a sunburn. After nine days of dolorous drifting, the tradewind returned and wafted them speedily westward. But so much fresh water had evaporated and so many stores had been spoiled that the Admiral decided to replenish in the Lesser Antilles before pursuing his search southerly. On 31 July he correctly estimated that he had reached the longitude "of the islands of the *Canibales*," and changed course to North by East, which was correct for Barbados or Tobago. This is a good example of his uncanny skill at dead-reckoning navigation, considering that he had seen no ships nor touched at known land for four weeks. At noon the same day (writes Columbus), "As the Divine Majesty has always shown mercy to me, a sailor climbed to the crow's nest and saw land westward in the shape of three mountains." To the Admiral and his men this landfall on three hills seemed miraculous, since he had dedicated this voyage to the Holy Trinity. So, naturally, he named the island Trinidad,

and at once altered his course to inspect it. Our first photograph (viii.1) shows Trinity Hills as he saw them; we flew out to the identical place of his landfall.

As the fleet proceeded, they made out a cape which the Admiral "called Cabo de la Galera from a great rock there which from a distance looked like a galley under sail." The resemblance to a big galley with three sails set and banks of oars is striking indeed. Our aërial close-up (viii.2) shows the diagonal rock strata, the edges of which at a distance suggest the long sweeps of a row-galley. This point is now called Cape Galeota.

viii.3

Columbus was abreast of this cape by evening and, as the moon was almost full, he decided to jog along westward, south of the Trinity Hills which he had seen from afar at noon (viii.3). Dawn on the first day of August revealed "groves of trees going right down to the sea" (viii.4), and close alongshore they sailed, to spy out a good anchorage where fresh water could be obtained. With his usual good judgment in such matters, the Admiral chose the best watering place on the south coast of Trinidad, behind a point which he called Punta de la Playa, and which has since been named Erin Point (viii.5) by some nostalgic exile from Ireland. Just around this point, on what is now called Frank Bay, a little stream empties into the ocean across a sand beach. Here the sailors, dehydrated in the doldrums, had a wonderful time drinking their fill of sweet, cool water, wallowing in the river, scraping

viii.4

their backs on the pebbles, washing their sweat-caked clothes, splashing each other, singing and shouting — but sunbathing, never! At least, we are sure they did; because seamen have always done just that in days of sail, after a long ocean voyage in which there was little opportunity to bathe. It was part of the old sea ritual.

Just before standing in for this bay, Columbus sighted to the southward something that looked like a flat island. This was Punta Bombeador (or, as some charts call it, Punta Pescadores) of Venezuela (viii.6). It was his first sight of the South American continent; but he supposed it was just another island, and named it Isla Sancta.

Next day, 2 August, the fleet rounded the southwestern point of Trinidad, which Columbus named Punta de Arena, and passed through the Boca de la

Sierpe or Serpent's Mouth, as he named it. In this *boca* Columbus observed the solitary rock now called Soldado, and named it El Gallo (The Cock). It does look like a proud little gamecock minus his head (viii.7).

Anchoring on the north side of Icacos Point in a shallow bay that has now been named Columbus Cove after him, the Admiral made his first contact with the natives of this region; and a bitter disappointment they were. Instead of silk-clad mandarins or sabled potentates, he found people similar in appearance to the Arawaks but who did not speak their language. They were largely naked, but the youths wore a sort of cotton bandanna of their own weaving, which reminded the Admiral of the *almaizar* kerchief which Moorish women in Spain imported from Africa. That was some consolation — surely a sign that these people traded with Africa around the back side of the world!

The first meeting with these natives had its comic side. A dugout paddled by about twenty-five men came within hailing distance of the fleet but refused to come aboard. Columbus then caused to be displayed some shiny brass chamber pots which he had brought as trading truck, having heard that these articles sold well in Africa. But the Indians had no use for chamber pots. So, hoping to amuse and attract them, he ordered a talented sailor to play on pipe and tabor, and the ship's boys to dance. This had the contrary effect from what he expected: the natives took it to be a war challenge

viii.7

and met it with a shower of arrows, which abruptly ended the pipe-and-dance routine. Columbus now ordered some crossbow bolts to be shot so as to go "plop" in the water near the canoe. These seemed to convince the natives that the Spaniards meant businesss, for they now approached and accepted the usual presents of beads, hawk's bells and red caps.

For two days the fleet remained off this beach north of Icacos Point (viii.8); the men fishing, gathering oysters and catching "parrots as big as domestic fowls"; and the Admiral sounding the Boca de la Sierpe and observing the currents. He had fortunately brought his fleet through at a time of slack water. But, just at their time of departure on 4 August, the seamen had the scare of their lives. "There came a current from the south as strong as a mighty flood, with such great noise and roar that it terrified all hands . . . and the ocean water . . . coming from the opposite direction caused the sea to rise, making a great and lofty tidal wave which tossed the flagship on its crest . . . and tripped the anchors of one of the other vessels (which ought already to have weighed), and forced her farther out to sea." This was not a tidal bore but a volcanic disturbance not uncommon in those waters; new islets are thrown up by such disturbances every few years. Whatever may have been the cause, it convinced Columbus that he could not hope to leave the Gulf the same way he came in, and his judgment is supported almost four centuries later by the *Sailing Directions for the West Indies*, which says, "Vessels never attempt sailing out of the Gulf by the Soldado or Southern Channel because of the current, which would render every attempt impracticable."

viii.9

After recovering from this shock, the fleet sailed North by East for about
fifty-five miles, straight across the Gulf of Paria, to investigate mountains
that appeared in that direction. In so doing they missed the fertile plains of
western Trinidad and the harbor of the future Port of Spain. They anchored for the night at Bahía Celeste (viii.9), inside Punta Peñas, the tip of
Paria Peninsula, which Columbus called Cabo de Lapa, Barnacle Cape; it has
a shape like those long-necked barnacles that attach themselves to ships. This
was his first mainland anchorage, but he did not go ashore, for he thought it
was just another big island, and gave it the name Isla de Gracia, Island of
Grace, as a logical supplement to the Island of the Trinity and the Holy Isle.
He did not yet suspect that of the three, Trinidad alone was insular.

As the Admiral looked around him from the poop deck that calm summer night, he saw to the southward a placid gulf, and to the eastward a succession of islands, between which flow the tidal passages still known by Columbus's name, Las Bocas del Dragón, The Dragon's Mouths. First came the island now named Chacachacare, which he named El Caracol, The Snail, on account of its shape; next came Huevos Island, which he called El Delfin, The Dolphin, and beyond that, Monos Island, which from a distance looks like a part of Trinidad; its blunt cape he called Cabo Boto (viii.10). Beyond Monos there showed up the mountainous part of Trinidad, with an outlying cape which he took to be an island and called Belaforma.

Postponing inspection of these islands and the bocas, Columbus decided to push westward along the south coast of the Paria Peninsula, looking for an exit around "Isla de Gracia." On Sunday, 5 August, he sailed south and west to a little scallop-shaped cove now called Ensenada Yacua, where a sand beach stretches a white ribbon between two rocky headlands (viii.11). Here he sent the boats ashore, and here, in this beautiful and quiet spot, little changed since his day, a European for the first time since the eleventh century set foot on the American continent. Columbus went into ecstasies over the beauty of this coast; and no wonder, for in their virgin state these shores were clothed densely with mahogany, manchineel, silk-cotton, butterwood, Christmas hope and other tropical trees. Brightly colored parrots and other birds screamed as they flew from tree to tree, and monkeys chattered among the boughs. But no Indians were about, so Columbus postponed taking possession until he found a spot complete with native witnesses.

At this point we run into a controversy that cannot be ignored — was Columbus the first to land on the continent? Amerigo Vespucci got the credit, owing to an alleged letter from him to Soderini, published in 1504, which de-

viii.11

AMERICA.

Americen Americus retexit, & *Semel vocauit inde femper excitam*

scribes a voyage of 1497 to Venezuela, and around the Gulf of Mexico and Florida. At best, this is a garbled and up-dated and extended version of Hojeda's voyage of 1499; but it struck the public fancy, as may be seen by this engraving of the Discovery of America by Johannes Stradanus done about 1580 (viii.12). Amerigo, nautical astrolabe in one hand and banner in the other, is surprising a very naked Carib lady in a hammock, who apparently was enjoying a siesta before indulging in a cannibalistic orgy. Thus the New World was named America, instead of Columbia, after its rightful discoverer. Simón Bolívar the Liberator attempted to redress this injustice by naming the first republic that he established in these regions La Gran Colombia. Subsequently Venezuela, Ecuador and Panama seceded from Great Colombia, leaving only the present Republic of Colombia in all South America to bear Columbus's name. Cabo Tiburón at the entrance of the Gulf of Darien is the only part of the present Colombia that Columbus discovered, and that was on his Fourth Voyage.

[159]

viii.13

To return to the Third Voyage of 1498 in the Gulf of Paria: the fleet weighed around noon and continued westward, passing more pretty coves like Ensenada Patao and anchoring for the night somewhere near the present Punta Juan Diego (viii.13). Next day, the 6th, resuming his westward course, he reached a big Indian village where a river flowed into the gulf. Its mouth is now blocked by a sand bar (viii.14), but Columbus was able to anchor within. This was the Río Guiría, where "many people came out, and told me," recorded Columbus, "that they called this land Paría." The Admiral went ashore with about fifty men and, sword in one hand and the royal standard in the other, took possession of this region in the name of Ferdinand and Isabella, and caused a cross to be set up — the first on the American continent.

Here the Spaniards had their first warm contact with the Guayquerí nation, belonging to a culture area extending from the Guianas to Honduras, hitherto untouched by Europeans. These Indians built big dugout canoes with a palm-thatched cabin amidships. They were expert weavers of scarves which Columbus thought to be imports from Africa, but not metallurgists. The gold and *guanín*[1] pendants showing birds, frogs or alligators that the Spaniards obtained here and called "eagles," were obtained by trade from the

[1] Columbus used this word, which modern archaeologists have replaced by *tumbaga*, for an alloy of gold and copper, the latter serving to lower the melting point.

viii.14

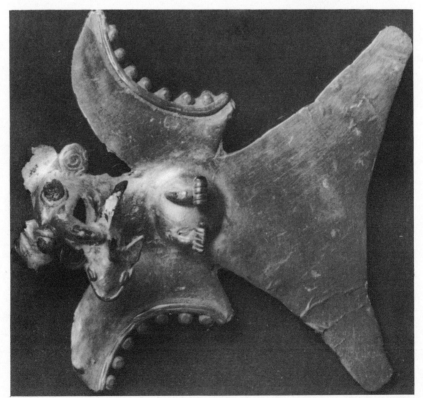

coast of Panama, where Columbus found an abundance on his Fourth Voyage (viii.15). The visitors were offered a drink fermented from maize and called *chicha*, which is still made in Venezuela and recently was forbidden in Colombia because some of the Indians were living on nothing else. The Spaniards liked the flavor of ripe sea grapes, the guava which they described "like oranges, with the inside like figs," *Spondias Mombin L.*, variously known as *caja, uvo, hubo* and hog plum, which grows all along the shores of the southern Caribbean (viii.16); the natives make jam of it today.

After spending two days at Guiría, Columbus continued westward. He rounded a sharp point which he called Punta del Aguja, Point of the Needle (viii.17). It is now named Punta Alcatraz, after the pelican, which abounds in the Gulf of Paria —"The pelican, whose bill can hold more than his belly can," as an old ditty describes him.

viii.17

Beyond Punta Alcatraz the coastline nowadays becomes a rich lowland covered with glossy-leaved tropical hardwood; in 1498 it was so well cultivated that Columbus named it Los Jardines, The Gardens (viii.18). He anchored there off a large village, where the natives created much excitement by coming out to the ships wearing necklaces of genuine pearls which, they rightly said, came from the other side of the peninsula. They were friendly, too, and entertained one boat's crew with *chicha* and native foods in a big house. Three or four days were spent in this pleasant place.

viii.18

On 10 August Columbus sailed past a point with high red bluffs, which answers the description of Punta Paparito (viii.19). His farthest west in the Gulf was a small harbor now called Irapa (viii.20). The water was now shoaling rapidly — less than three fathoms off Irapa — and becoming so fresh

viii.19

that Columbus, suspecting the mouth of a great river to be near, sent his smallest caravel, *El Correo*, to explore westward. She rejoined the fleet after a day or two, reporting that she had found "a vast gulf and four large openings therein . . . and at the end of each of them a river." These were the four mouths of the Río Grande, northernmost branch of the Orinoco; and we may give Captain Hernán Pérez of *Correo* the credit for having discovered that mighty river.

viii.20

It took Columbus a few days to sort out these unexpected facts and decide that he had touched a continent. Already he realized that he could not get out to sea this way; so he reversed course, and with a fair wind and a favoring current passed The Gardens, Punta Alcatraz and Ensenada Yacua, and anchored for the night of 12 August in a harbor of Chacachacare Island which he called Puerto de Gatos (viii.21), after the monkeys that amused the sailors by chattering angrily at them when they came ashore. Columbus followed Marco Polo in calling monkeys *gatos paulos*, "Paul cats," as distinct from ordinary tomcats, to which they thought monkeys were related. He

[165]

viii.21

sent a boat to investigate a tiny harbor in nearby Heuvos Island, where the men found some native fishermen's huts, so Columbus named it Puerto de las Cabañas — Cabin Harbor (viii.22).

The Admiral now had a choice of four channels through which to leave the

viii.22

Gulf: Monos, Huevos, Navios, and Grande, as they are called today. Wisely he chose the last-named as the widest; it is shown in our photograph of Monkey Harbor. In mid-channel the three caravels had plenty of trouble, owing to the turmoil created between the fresh water from the Orinoco flowing out and the salt tide pressing in, "so furious and violent that it raised a great tidal bore with a very high crest" that roared frightfully. It was as bad as the volcanic disturbance near the Boca de la Sierpe, and more dangerous; for the wind died away, no anchor could reach bottom, the current slewed the ships around, and threatened to cast them on the rocks. Eventually the layer of fresh water on top of the salt swept them out to the broad Caribbean. Columbus then named his exit La Boca Dragón, The Dragon's Mouth, as it is to this day.

Now, taking advantage of a light westerly, the Admiral made a wide sweep to the east and north, sighting from afar Tobago and Grenada, as we have observed in Chapter VII. Leaving Grenada far distant on the starboard hand, he again closed the Paria Peninsula in order to resume his search for the strait which was not there, between it and the Gulf.

Columbus, during this second week of August, although suffering from arthritis and severe headaches, was putting the facts of his recent discoveries into fresh prophecies and a new geographical pattern. In his Journal he wrote, "Your Highnesses have won these vast lands which are an Other World (*que son Otro Mundo*), in which Christendom will have so much enjoyment and our faith in time so great an increase." And, "I have come to believe that this is a mighty continent which was hitherto unknown. I am greatly supported in this view by reason of this great river." In a letter to the Sovereigns of 18 October 1498, he further develops the theory that this entire region, from its beauty and amenity and the great river, must be the Terrestrial Paradise from which Adam and Eve were expelled. "Your Highnesses have an Other World here," he wrote. By *Otro Mundo* it must not be inferred that Columbus grasped the correct relation of his discoveries to the Old World; he merely meant (as Vespucci did when, later, he called the same regions *Mundus Novus*) that it was a world unknown to the ancients or to Ptolemy. Columbus never abandoned his theory that Cuba was a cape of southeast China, or that west and south of it lay the "Golden Chersonese," the Malay Peninsula.

viii.23

South and Central America, from Paria to Honduras, he believed to be a newly discovered continent tailing off from the Malay Peninsula much as Indonesia actually does; and the main object of his next voyage was to find a strait between them.

Sailing westward, Columbus discovered a group of low islands that he called Los Testigos (viii.23), a name that has survived, and a pinnacle rock that he named El Romero, The Pilgrim, and is now called La Sola (viii.24).

viii.24

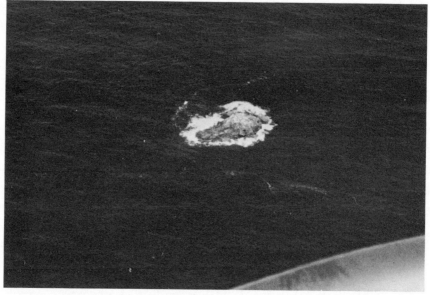

Next he sighted another group of islets that he called Las Guardias, probably because they suggested sentinels of the big island Margarita, which may be seen in the background of our photograph (viii.25). They are now called Los Frailes, the Friars. At the same time he obtained distant views of three

viii.25

prominent capes on the Paria Peninsula, which he named Rico, De Sabor and Luengo. It is anyone's guess which these are on the modern map; we in Six-zero-Papa picked out, as most likely to have attracted the Admiral's attention, the most prominent: Tres Puntas (viii.26), Chagurema and Malapascua[1]

[1] Meaning "Bad Christmas," doubtless reflecting an unfortunate experience of some later Spaniard.

viii.26

viii.27

(viii.27). The fourth cape, which Columbus called Cabo de Conchas, we believe to be the modern Cabo Escudo Blanco; white marks on the rocks having looked like shells to the Admiral, and shields to later Spaniards. We could see neither shells nor shields, and the lighter spots on our photograph are yellow (viii.28). But perhaps the white areas were guano, which the rain washed off when European cultivation drove sea birds to offshore islands like La Sola.

viii.28

From Cabo Escudo Blanco one can look up the Gulf of Cubagua between Margarita and the Cumaná Peninsula and see the island of Coche and distant Cubagua (viii.29). Columbus knew from what the natives told him on the other side of the peninsula that this was their source of pearls, but he did not investigate it, because he was in a desperate hurry to reach Santo Domingo, and thought that the pearls could wait. That was a bad mistake. When Columbus's flagship returned to Spain without him in October, it carried his chart, on which this center of the pearl fisheries was indicated; and that merry scamp Alonso de Hojeda, a favorite of the Queen, not only borrowed the chart but obtained permission to organize a voyage of his own to Cubagua. On this voyage of 1499 he obtained bushels of fine pearls for a song.

viii.29

The great island of Margarita, which we show as seen between the sails of our *Capitana* in 1939 (viii.30), was so called by Columbus after the Infanta Margarita of Austria. This little lady was a beauty and a wit. Affianced at the age of seventeen to Charles VIII of France, who jilted her, she was then betrothed to the Prince of the Asturias, heir to the Spanish throne. In the course of a violent storm on her voyage from Flanders to marry Don Juan in Spain, she composed an epitaph for herself: —

> *Ci gît Margot, la gentille demoiselle*
> *Qui a deux maris et encore est pucelle.*

viii.30

Fortunately she survived the perils of the sea; and Columbus, who had provided the weather forecast for the nuptial voyage and attended the state wedding, had the happy thought to name this beautiful island of smiling valleys between tumbled mountains (viii.31) after the plucky little princess.

viii.31

He never set foot on Margarita. On 15 August, leaving it on the port hand and Los Frailes to starboard and sighting the island of Blanquilla (viii.32), he sailed cautiously across the Caribbean, heaving-to at night for fear of running afoul of islands or reefs, since it was the dark of the moon. On the 20th he made landfall on the prominent outlying rock Alta Vela which we have depicted (see v.41, page 106). In the harbor behind Beata Island he met his brother Bartholomew. They cruised upwind in company, and the Admiral's Third Voyage ended at Santo Domingo on 31 August 1498.

This, in the long view, was his most successful voyage after the First. He had discovered the mainland, the island of Trinidad, a mouth of the Orinoco, and the country later named Venezuela; lands of such beauty, mild climate and potential wealth that his notion of having found the Terrestrial Paradise does not seem unreasonable. But he was bitterly disappointed in not having exploited the pearl fisheries behind Margarita, which would have enhanced his credit at court and might well have prevented later humiliation at the hands of his enemies.

viii.32

CHAPTER IX

Honduras, Nicaragua and Costa Rica

FOLLOWING Columbus's Third Voyage, in which he discovered the American continent, there had been several explorations of the mainland of South America. Pedr'alvares Cabral and Vicente Yañez Pinzón discovered different parts of Brazil in 1500, and Amerigo Vespucci, probably under the Portuguese Coelho, pushed south, possibly as far as the River Plate. Alonso de Hojeda and Rodrigo de Bastídas took up the exploration of the Spanish Main where Columbus left off in 1498, and the latter probably got as far as the Gulf of Darien. But nobody had yet discovered the mainland of Central America, or sailed into the western Caribbean or the Gulf of Mexico. Columbus, assuming (as we have seen) that South America was in about the same relative position to the Malay Peninsula as Indonesia, believed that if he explored this yet unknown coast he would find a strait to the Indian Ocean. There must be one; for hadn't Marco Polo sailed through the Strait of Malacca? That high authorities shared his bizarre theory of a shrunken globe and a narrow, single ocean is proved by the fact that Columbus carried a letter of introduction from Ferdinand and Isabella to Vasco da Gama, the Portuguese discoverer who had left in 1502 on his second voyage to India via the Cape of Good Hope. "Since by good hap you may meet by sea" — i.e., in the Indian Ocean, reads this letter, "we have commanded Admiral D. Christopher Columbus that if you two meet, you should treat one another as friends." Unfortunately, the presence of a continent and an unknown ocean several thousand miles wide prevented a shipboard conference between the two greatest navigators of the century.

The mainland part of Columbus's Fourth and last voyage began on 1 August 1502, when his four caravels, *La Capitana, Santiago de Palos, El Gallego* and *El Vizcaíno*,[1] reached the coast of Honduras, and ended on 1 May 1503, when, with the first two only, he took off from Cabo Tiburón, Colombia, for Jamaica. These ten months were packed with so much adventure, so many struggles against the elements, such surprising discoveries, fierce fights and marine disasters, that the Admiral called this Fourth Voyage *El Alto Viaje*, the High Voyage. Columbus's own journal has not survived, but his letters have; and, fortunately for us, his son Ferdinand, thirteen years old when the voyage began, accompanied his father and wrote a detailed account in his biography of the Admiral.

The fleet crossed the Caribbean from off the south coast of Cuba, and on 30 July 1502 raised Bonacca, one of the Bay Islands off Honduras. Columbus used the native name Guanari; it is now officially Guanaja. We agree with the report of a certain Lieutenant Smith of the Royal Navy, made a century ago, that Bonacca "seems to have undergone little change since its first discovery. Its magnificent forests still please the eye of the mariner, as they did 300 years since, and the scenery is seldom surpassed. The highest lands have cohune and pine ridges, with spots of white granite here and there visible between the trees, with bold cliffs of red and yellow ochre making a varied and pleasing landscape from seaward. Its harbours are excellent, with channels in so many directions as to be accessible for the largest ships in any wind" (ix.1). Anchoring in one of these — we have no means of telling which — Columbus found the shores to be inhabited by Jicaque Indians, or the kindred Paya, nations long since driven from the coast, and whose survivors now live in a reservation in the mountains.

The fleet had not been there long before a very big dugout canoe, paddled by 25 men, entered the harbor. Ferdinand described her as "all of one tree, long as a galley," and of proportionate beam. Within it and admidships, reminding him of the cabin of a Venetian gondola, was "a shelter made of palm leaves," under which "were the children, the cargo and trading truck

---

[1] See note 1 to Chapter I on the names of Spanish ships. The flagship's real name was *Santa María*. *Santiago's* nickname was *Bermuda*, after her owner Juan Bermudez. *Gallego* (The Galician) and *Vizcaíno* (The Biscayan) were both nicknames; we do not know what their real names were. These were all small, handy caravels which Columbus preferred for exploration. *La Capitana*, the biggest, was even smaller than *Niña*.

ix.1

. . . such as quilts and sleeveless shirts of cotton, embroidered and dyed in several colors and designs . . . and sheets in which the Indian women aboard the canoe wrapped themselves, like the Moorish women of Granada." There were wooden swords with cutting edges of flint, copper hatchets and crucibles, a supply of the fermented drink *chicha* which the Spaniards had enjoyed in Venezuela, and nuts, which the Indians so valued that when they dropped one, "all stooped to pick it up, as if an eye had fallen from their heads." The colored jumpers are still made along this coast, as our photograph of a San Blas child shows (ix.2), although the color now is provided by appliqué work rather than embroidery. The nuts were cacao beans; Samuel de Champlain, late in that century, found these being used as currency in Mexico at the rate of sixty to a real, or five to a penny. The Indians who plied this enormous canoe were from the Honduran mainland, probably bound for Yucatán, where the Maya, whose forte was not metal working, set great store by the work of Jicaque metallurgists. Columbus helped himself to samples of the canoe cargo, and detained as interpreter an old man named Iumbe or Guimbe.

The long arm of Spain never again reached these Bay Islands. They formed part of the Old Providence colony established by the Earl of Warwick in the early seventeenth century, and which evolved into a British crown colony.

[176]

England finally ceded the Bay Islands to Honduras in 1859, greatly to the displeasure of the inhabitants, who were largely the descendants of British buccaneers. They still speak English, and those of Bonacca live sociably on one big cay to avoid, it is said, the insect life of the big island.

Columbus now made for Cape Honduras on the mainland, visible from Bonacca. Columbus called it Punta Caxinas, after the Arawak name of a tree growing there in abundance, *Chrysobalanus icaco* (ix.3),[1] which in Cuba he had falsely identified as Marco Polo's coconut. The cape is now called Punta Castilla, but the older name Cape Honduras survives on charts. It is a long, low point, now covered by green scrub. Rounding it, you enter a noble and spacious harbor, Trujillo Bay, where Hernán Cortés founded the city of Trujillo around 1524; it became the metropolis of Spanish Honduras and the seat of a bishop as early as 1539. Behind the town the Vigia and Calentura

[1] See engraving of the tree (iv.14, page 54).

.2

ix.3

peaks rise to 2500 feet (ix.4). It was at Trujillo that the famous filibuster William Walker met his death at the hands of a Honduran firing squad. Fifty years ago, Trujillo Bay was an important center of banana export for the Honduras plantations; but the banana trees in this region have suffered from blight, and the city, having only a dirt road and mule-trail connection with the interior, has become a depressed area.

At anchor in Trujillo Bay, where he tarried for a week or more, Columbus pondered whether he would pursue his search for The Strait westward or eastward. Had he turned west, he should have made the Yucatán Peninsula (of whose existence the Indians had told him), and thus contacted the highly civilized Maya. He decided against the western route, says Ferdinand, because he believed he could do that best from Cuba on another voyage, and felt that he must cover the unknown coast between Trujillo and Darien. He must also have realized that a westerly course would take him even farther to leeward, and increase the difficulty of beating back home against wind and current if he found no strait to the Indian Ocean; and, of course, there was an equal chance of finding a strait in the easterly direction. A wretched time he had in the attempt.

At the beginning of the second week of August 1502, the fleet rounded Cape Honduras and started eastward on what turned out to be the most uncomfortable and exhausting sail of Columbus's career. On Sunday the 14th

ix.4

they anchored off the mouth of a river, and "the Adelantado [Bartholomew] with the banners, the captains and many of the fleet" landed and heard mass said by Fray Alixandro, the fleet chaplain; possibly the first mass ever celebrated on the mainland. It seems odd that mass was not celebrated earlier at Trujillo Bay. Possibly Fray Alixandro was indisposed, as he seems to have been during the rest of the voyage. On 17 August Columbus went ashore to take formal possession for his Sovereigns, and so named the place Río de la Posesión. We identify this river mouth as that of the Romano or Aguán, where the English later set up an important trading post (ix.5). Ferdinand records that "the country was green and fair, although low," which suits the valley of the Romano, whilst the sierra closely approaches the sea at the more easterly river mouths. Ferdinand adds that there were "plenty of pines, oaks, palm trees of several kinds, and myrobolans, the sort that in Hispaniola are called *hobi*," [1] as well as "many leopards, deer and gazelles." These animals naturally aroused great interest among the Spaniards, because in the islands and on Paria they had seen no quadruped bigger than the hutía. The leopards were obviously jaguars or pumas; the·deer and gazelles were evidently the stags and fawns of the small red deer that is hunted in Honduras today.

The Indians here, assured by Iumbe that the Christians could be trusted,

[1] *Spondias Mombin L.* See photograph (viii.16, page 162).

were wary but friendly, furnishing the fleet with flesh, fish, fowl, beans, and other provisions. Significantly, Ferdinand does not mention maize, for the Jicaque Indians, to the surprise of later Spaniards, did not cultivate maize. They were heavily tattooed and painted "to appear beautiful," noted Ferdinand, "but actually they look like the devil." Through holes in their ears they fastened gold ornaments shaped like an hourglass (ix.6), and from these ear-spools hung heavy gold disks which elongated their ear lobes. For that reason, says Ferdinand, his father named this coast La Costa de las Orejas.

ix.6

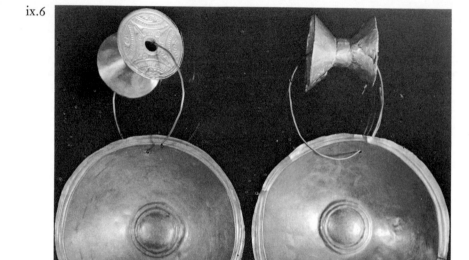

This coastal country of Honduras and Nicaragua, which once supported Indian nations who lived well and practiced the arts, is now very depressed. The logwood and mahogany forests on the upper reaches of the rivers, which the English used to pay the Indians to fell and float downstream, have been denuded; the banana plantations have been devastated by the "Panama disease," and such Indians as have not retired to the mountains live largely by fishing. Ships no longer call at the harbors and river mouths once frequented by British timber carriers; from Six-oh-Papa we sighted but one small boat between Cape Honduras and Cape Gracias a Dios. Cabo Camarón (ix.7) is the only outstanding promontory. Just east of it is the mouth of the Río Negro (formerly called the Tinto), which we photographed (ix.8), because several historians of this region believe it, rather than the Romano, to have been Columbus's Río de la Posesión.[1]

After three days at Río de la Posesión, the fleet resumed an eastward course. It encountered head winds the entire way, taking four weeks to make good about 210 miles, keeping close to shore and anchoring every night. Columbus did this because, rightly suspecting the existence of offshore cays, he dared not sail at night; and also, possibly he feared missing an entrance to The Strait. It was gusty, rainy weather, the crew were miserable, and so expectant of a watery death that they began hearing one another's confessions

[1] To this theory we do not subscribe (1) because the Negro lies a scant 150 miles, as against the Romano's 210 miles, from Cape Gracias a Dios, so that the four weeks' sailing that Columbus required to reach that cape from Río de la Posesión is much more likely to have commenced at the more westerly river; and (2) because the coastal plain is much narrower at the Negro than at the Romano.

—Fray Alixandro apparently being too seasick to function. The Admiral, suffering from arthritis, was unable to move, and conned his flagship from a *camarilla*, a doghouse that the people built for him on the poop deck. "Other tempests have I seen," wrote Columbus, "but none that lasted so long or so grim as this."

What made matters worse was the nature of this land, now called the Miskito Coast. It is the most dismal coast ever seen by Columbus — or by us of

ix.8

Six-oh-Papa. Behind a seemingly endless sand beach on which breakers continually roar (ix.9) is a series of shallow, stagnant lagoons which abound in fish, oysters and shrimp, and afford a livelihood of sorts to the descendants of the Miskito or Zambo, a hybrid group developed in the seventeenth century by the crossing of Paya, Kurkra and Sumo Indians with escaped Negro slaves. Up in the hills there are fertile savannahs where cattle are bred and wild horses roam, but within sight of the shore there are few signs of human or animal life; only windblown stunted trees, muddy, meandering river mouths, mangroves and stagnant lagoons (ix.10) so thick with the water hyacinth and other weeds that canoes get through with difficulty (ix.11).

ix.11

[183]

As every sailor knows, fair weather follows foul, bad luck changes to good. In this case the good arrived on 14 September, when the fleet, after weathering False Cape and its nasty outlying reefs, doubled a promontory from which the coast trended almost due south. Now the caravels could romp along under a clear sky with wind on the port beam; so Columbus named this point of deliverance Cabo Gracias a Dios, Cape Thanks Be to God (ix.12). It retains that name to this day, although Bartholomew Columbus in his sketch map called it Punta de Consuelo; i.e., Point of Consolation.

The Coco or Wanks river, navigable by small craft for some 150 miles, bisects Cape Gracias a Dios; the left bank belongs to Honduras and the right to Nicaragua, which maintains a customs official at what the 1872 *Sailing Directions* describes as "a small, rude village" near the mouth. It is even smaller and presumably ruder today, with but one little trading sloop at anchor when we flew over in October 1963. The lower reaches of the river have become so difficult to navigate that cargoes of logs, chicle, rubber and rice are unloaded up river at a modern town called Waspán, which is connected with Puerto Cabezas by road.

From Gracias a Dios to Puerto Limón, Columbus's fleet enjoyed not only fair wind but protection from numerous outlying cays. Since most of the trading along this coast for two centuries or more was done by the English and their colonists, the cays and channels have English names such as Archie, the Witties, the Hobbies, Man-of-War, and Corn; and the Zambos who inhabit these and the adjacent mainland speak English or Miskito rather than Spanish. All this coast, known as the Mosquito Protectorate or Mosquitia, was under British jurisdiction until 1860, when, owing largely to pressure by the United States, it was ceded to Nicaragua.

The fleet passed a bold red clay headland, now called Bragmans Bluff, land-mark for the seaport of Puerto Cabezas (ix.13). On 16 September they anchored off the mouth of a river, "that seemed to have a good entrance," to get firewood and sweet water, which was lacking in the muddy, sluggish rivers they had seen for the past month. Columbus sent his boats over the bar

ix.13

safely, "But the coming out proved not so; for the sea breeze blew up strong and the waves ran high against the current of the river, so strongly assaulting the boats that one of them was lost with all hands. Therefore the Admiral called it the Río de los Desastres." We identified this as the Río Grande, 120 miles south of Cape Gracias a Dios (ix.14). Off its mouth today there is a

ix.14

ix.15

semicircular breaking bar which the chart labels "dangerous," and certainly looks it. Once inside, small craft can navigate this river for some 150 miles.

During the following weeks, Columbus's fleet skirted this Miskito coast of the future Republic of Nicaragua for about 130 miles, probably anchoring every night, since fair anchorage is to be found in many places along that shore. They rounded a promontory that Captain Porras called Cabo de Rojas, which must have been Bluefields Bluff with its red cliffs. They passed prominent Punta Mona or Monkey Point (ix.15), crossed the shallow Bahía de San Juan del Norte, passing the mouth of the like-named river (ix.16).

The San Juan del Norte was the most important river that Columbus passed on this voyage. Neither Ferdinand nor any other person who described this voyage mentions a river that can be identified with the San Juan, so it is

ix.16

probable that the fleet sailed by in the night. Columbus missed his chance of a lifetime to find the Strait. His smaller caravels could have sailed up the San Juan to Lake Nicaragua, whose western shore, at one point, is only fifteen miles from the Pacific. In the colonial era trading vessels used to sail right up the river to the lake, where Spain built a port of entry. Earthquakes later rendered the San Juan less navigable; yet, at the time of the California gold rush of 1850, "Commodore" Vanderbilt was able to send small steamers up to the lake. There was great activity here in the last century when the digging of a Nicaragua Canal was actively planned, and even begun. Miskito Indians in 1848 seized the settlement that the English called Greytown at the mouth of the river and annexed it to the Mosquito protectorate. Disorders broke out there in 1854, and in retaliation for the American minister to Nicaragua being wounded by a flying bottle, U.S.S. *Cyane* bombarded and largely destroyed the town — an incident which might have led to war if Britain had not then been involved in the Crimea. She finally washed her hands of local responsibilities by ceding Mosquitia to Nicaragua in 1860. Greytown, renamed San Juan del Norte, enjoyed another boom in the 1880's when the canal project was revived; but the choice of the Panama route killed all activity, and the town has shrunk to a tiny village which we could barely see from Six-zero-Papa.

On 25 September Columbus's fleet reached a region which the Indians called Cariay, and spent ten days anchored behind a charmingly wooded islet which the natives called Quiriviri and the Admiral named La Huerta, The Garden. This can certainly be identified as Uvita islet (ix.17), and the place is

ix.17

ix.18 modern Puerto Limón, Costa Rica. Señor Juan E. Romagosa S., former harbor master of Puerto Limón, has even figured out exactly where Columbus would have moored his fleet in order to obtain best protection from the trade-wind; so, in 1940, we anchored our *Capitana* in the same place (ix.18).

Puerto Limón being the first good harbor that the fleet had found since its exhausting beat along the "Coast of Ears," the Admiral decided to give his people a good rest. The indications are that they enjoyed themselves thoroughly among the natives, who hunted the deer and the jaguar, which the Christians thought to be a kind of leopard. These Cariay Indians, besides being expert metallurgists, made some excellent pottery, of which we show a specimen depicting one of themselves fighting a jaguar with an enormous stone ax (ix.19).

ix.19

After the fleet came to an anchor off the future Puerto Limón, a great concourse of Indians gathered on the shore, armed with bows and arrows, spears and clubs. The men wore their hair braided and wound about their heads, and both they and the women wore "eagles" of guanín pendent around their necks, "as we do an *Agnus Dei* or other reliquary," wrote Ferdinand (ix.20). The Admiral kept his people on board, fearing trouble; but the Cariay were so eager to trade that many swam out to the caravels carrying a line of cotton jumpers and guanín ornaments. Columbus, inexplicably, refused to barter but sent his visitors ashore laden with gifts. The Indians then tried an ancient method of persuading unwilling traders to do business. They sent out to the flagship two virgins, one about eight, the other about fourteen years old. "The damsels," says Ferdinand, "showed great fortitude; for despite the Christians' being complete strangers to them in appearance, manners and race, they gave no signs of grief or fear, but always looked cheerful and modest. The Admiral showed them good usage; he had them clothed and fed, and

ix.20

then ordered them to be set ashore . . . and the old man who had delivered them received them again with much rejoicing." But the Admiral, in his Letter to the Sovereigns, says that the two girls behaved "with such lack of modesty as to be no better than whores." Why not give these Talamanca virgins the benefit of the doubt?

As Iumbe the interpreter had been allowed to go home in his canoe from Cape Gracias a Dios, since he could no longer understand the language, the Christians captured two Cariay to train as interpreters. Columbus noted "many fowls of great size, having feathers like wool"; these were the *kusu* or Currasow bird, a species of wild turkey which the Indians of Costa Rica still domesticate (ix.21). He was presented with a peccary, the wild boar of that

ix.21

region, so fierce that on board the flagship he chased an Irish wolfhound around the deck. One of the men who had been hunting ashore then brought in a spider monkey which he had shot down alive, with one foreleg gone. Since baiting animals against each other was then considered good sport, and the wolfhound refused to face the peccary, the Admiral caused the monkey to be thrown at him. Monkey wound his tail around piggy's snout and bit him until he screamed with pain. "This novel and pretty sport," as Columbus called it, he described in detail in his Letter to the Sovereigns, knowing that if Queen Isabella did not appreciate it, King Ferdinand would.

We may conclude this chapter with a photograph of Six-zero-Papa being refueled at Puerto Limón's charming airport on the edge of the sea (ix.22).

ix.22

CHAPTER X

Panama and Colombia

THE FLEET tarried ten days at Puerto Limón. On 5 October it made sail along the coast southeasterly, and found a channel opening into a great bay. Was this The Strait? Alas, no; it was only a passage, now known as La Boca del Dragón, leading to a great bay of the Republic of Panama which Columbus called by its native name Ceradaró or Zorobarú. It is now called Almirante after him (x.1). "The people nearby on the shore were all naked as they had come out of their mothers' wombs, and they had only a gold mirror about the neck, and some an eagle of guanín," wrote Ferdinand. "They immediately gave a gold mirror which weighed ten ducats in exchange for three hawk's bells." As a ducat weighed about 3.5 grams or $2.50 in gold,

X.1

and hawk's bells cost only a penny or two, this was a profitable trade indeed; the Indians assured the Spaniards that there was more gold eastward. The gold disk from the Robert Woods Bliss collection which we show here is an example of what the Spaniards called mirrors. It is 10½ inches in diameter (x.2). These and the "eagles" were the most valuable gold objects that they had yet encountered, and some even bigger ones were obtained at the same rate a few days later.

X.2

Columbus now felt that he was getting really warm on his search for The Strait. Quiriquetana, as the Indians called this region, he assumed to be Ciamba, Marco Polo's name for Cochin China; and the spacious gestures that they used to describe the next bay he assumed to mean the Indian Ocean. So, on 6 October he hopefully sailed through a strait so narrow that the foliage of the trees brushed the rigging of the caravels. This we have identified as Split Hill

Channel in which, prior to the earthquake of 1912, there were 14 feet of water (x.3).

Again, this was no passage to India. It led into the spacious Laguna de Chiriquí, which Columbus called by its native name Aburema. Chiriquí is a beautiful sheet of peacock-hued water, an inland lake 30 miles long and 15 wide, cupped in a verdure-clad cordillera which rises 12,000 feet above sea level. A profitable trade with the Indians who dwelt on its shores went briskly on; and through interpreters from Puerto Limón, who learned Castilian with surprising rapidity, Columbus gathered both geographical truth and fable. They told him that he was on an isthmus between two seas, the southern lying nine days' march across the cordillera. The Spaniards were actually but fifty miles from the Pacific — as the crow flies — and nine days would have been little enough to cross that heavy jungle, which even now can be traversed only by a narrow trail. The fabulous part was a series of tall tales about the natives of Ciguare, as they called the province on the other side of the mountains. The Ciguarians wore rich garments, built warships armed with cannon, and used cavalry in battle! (One wonders how an Indian who had never seen a horse described cavalry to a Spaniard.) A great river, which Columbus assumed to be the Ganges, lay only ten days' sail from Ciguare. This mixture of truth and myth seems to have convinced the Admiral that there was no strait, only an isthmus; and that was correct. But, as we shall see, a little more enterprise around Christmastide might have suggested that the isthmus could be crossed.

Ten days the fleet spent exploring and trading in Chiriquí Lagoon; the last few, probably, in Bluefield Creek (x.4), a harbor so beautiful that even the *Central America and Mexico Pilot* raves about the scenery. On 17 October, choosing a day of westerly wind, the Admiral stood out to sea, rounded Cape Valiente and passed a little island shaped like a Spanish escutcheon which he named El Escudo; it is still called El Escudo de Veragua (x.5). They were now in the harborless Golfo de los Mosquitos, the northern verge of the Province of Veragua. That was a native name, latinized, from which the descendants of Columbus take their title. For in 1536 the Discoverer's daughter-in-law Doña Maria de Colón y Toledo renounced, on behalf of her son Don Luis Colón, the "third Admiral," and his descendants, their ancestral claim to govern the entire Spanish Indies, in return for a pension, an absolute

x.4

[195]

x.5

grant of this region, and the titles Duke of Veragua and Marquess of Jamaica. These titles the lineal descendants of Don Luis still use; but the Duchy of Veragua is a mere province or department of the Republic of Panama.

Veragua is one great mountain chain covered with tropical rain forest. The steep part of the cordillera, which rises to over 6000 feet, ends between ten and thirty miles from the sea, the interval being covered by an undulating peneplain, also covered by thick jungle. Rainfall is so heavy that every few miles there is a river which empties into the Caribbean, building up a bar at its mouth; the first that we encountered was the Río Chiriquí (x.6). The scenery is magnificent, even stupendous, but inhuman. A thin lip of silt at the river mouths is used by a sparse and poor population to grow corn and a few coconuts and bananas. The people can get about only by canoe or jungle trail; roads are nonexistent. Señora de Obregón's photograph of a hundred-foot red cliff, now called El Frontón de Gaupán (x.7), gives a good idea of the lush, dark-green tropical vegetation, among which certain trees thrust up great racemes of mauve or bright yellow blossoms.

x.6

Columbus's fleet, approaching this coast at the Frontón or at another red cliff, the nearby Punta Peñasco (x.8), called at a number of villages on or near the river mouths Ferdinand says were named Cativa, Cobraba and Urira, but their exact location cannot now be determined. After passing these, they came to the village called Veragua at the mouth of the like-named river. At every place the natives rushed down to the beach, howling, spitting, beating drums, blowing conch-shell trumpets, and brandishing spears at the visitors. The conch shell, which served the Indians as war horn throughout America — our illustration (x.9) is from Father Sahagun's illustrated book on Mexico of about 1560 — emits a hideous, high-pitched shriek which, when coupled with war cries and accompanied by drums, creates a truly terrifying din. The imperturbable Spaniards countered with a few cannon shots, which brought the Indians "to reason," and yielded a rich haul of gold disks and pendants. Columbus did not know that he had run into a group of Indians who vie with the Araucanians of Chile and the Iroquois of North America as the toughest fighters in the New World. Ethnologists are not agreed as to what nation of Indians these belong to, so we simply call them the Veraguas.

The Admiral did not tarry here in October 1502, as he wished to take advantage of an unusually fair wind to cover the coast eastward. But he marked it down as the most likely place to obtain a quantity of gold. He was right about that; there is plenty of gold in Veragua today, but the frequent freshets, washing down into the Caribbean any sluice-boxes or other means of catching the precious metal, have prevented exploitation on a commercial scale.

After a tempestuous voyage to the Gulf of San Blas and back, the Admiral pitched on the mouth of a river called Yebra by the natives, which he named Río de Belén (of Bethlehem), because he reached it on the Epiphany, 6 January 1503. This Río Belén, still so called (x.10), lies between the Río Escribanos and the Río Veragua — only a mile and a quarter from the former, and two miles and a half from the latter. It is difficult to distinguish one from the other, and all charts are inaccurate; but Morison, by examining the region closely from a small boat in 1940, and questioning the natives, is confident that he has straightened out the puzzle. A prominent landmark for the Belén is the saddle-shaped mountain called La Silla de Veragua, and for the Veragua there is a curiously cleft summit which sailors call The Fox's Ears or Bishop's Mitre, each mountain being 15 to 18 miles from the sea. Low-lying clouds concealed their summits from Six-zero-Papa.

X.10

The bar at the mouth of the Belén cannot now be crossed by anything bigger than a canoe, but when Columbus arrived there were six or seven feet of water over it, and he had no trouble getting his four caravels over and into a basin with room for a dozen ships. So the Admiral decided to stay until the rainy season was over, and to use Belén as headquarters for exploring Veragua; but it rained almost without stopping for over a month.

In the meantime Bartholomew Columbus, taking the ships' boats and some seventy men, had rowed up the Río Veragua where he made friendly contact with the Veraguan cacique known as El Quibián (The Big Chief), and discovered gold deposits being worked by the Indians. They made no objection to the Christians digging there for four hours. Every man got his whack of gold dust; and one, a Jew (records Bartholomew), secured a little bag of gold that weighed two marks — 16 ounces. The men returned to their ships highly delighted, and anticipating vast riches; this was the highest point of the High Voyage.

The discovery of the gold mine, together with El Quibián's assurance that it was a mere token of what his territory contained, determined Columbus to establish a trading post inside the mouth of the Belén, to leave his brother there with a garrison, sail home with the good news, and return with reinforcements. On a *montecillo,* a little hillock beside the basin, now easily identified (x.11), the men began building a village that the Admiral christened Santa María de Belén. By the time ten or twelve houses had been erected, the

X.11

river level dropped, the bar was exposed, and the caravels could not get out; so, as Ferdinand quaintly remarks, "we had nothing left but to commend ourselves to God and pray for rain, as before we had prayed for fair weather."

At this juncture there came that inevitable change of attitude on the part of American Indians when they realized that the white men, tolerable as visiting traders, meant to settle down. Small parties of Veraguas in war-like array began skulking around the settlement; it looked like bad business. Columbus sent Diego Méndez, gentleman volunteer in *Santiago*, and Rodrigo d'Escobar, a ship's boy of *Vizcaíno*, to the Quibián's headquarters up the Río Veragua, to try and smoke out the cacique's intentions. Diego's report of this reconnaissance gives such an extraordinary instance of Spanish courage and coolness that we are giving it in full: —

"I found them all in battle array, and they would not let me go to the principal residence of the cacique. So I, pretending that I had come as a surgeon to cure him of a wound in his leg, and through dint of handing out gifts, they let me go to the royal residence, which stood on a flat-topped hill where there was a large plaza whose stockade was decorated with 300 heads of the men he had killed in battle. Then, after I had passed through the plaza and had reached the royal house, there was a great outcry from the women and boys standing at the door. They ran screaming into the palace and a son of the cacique came out in great rage, spitting out angry words in his own language. He laid hands on me and with one big push shoved me far from him. To calm him down I said I had come to heal his father's leg and showed him a curious ointment I had brought for this purpose. He replied that in no case could I enter where his father was. Seeing that I could not appease him that way, I whipped out a comb, a pair of scissors, and a mirror, and made Escobar, my companion, comb my hair and cut it. This really astonished him and the others who were there. I then got him [the cacique's son] to let Escobar comb his hair and cut it with the scissors; and I presented him with the scissors, the comb and the brush, and that made him friendly. I then asked for some food. This they brought immediately and we ate and drank in harmony and good fellowship like friends. Thereupon I left him and came to the ships and made a full report of all this to the Admiral, my lord, who took no little pleasure in learning of all these matters and the things which I had done."

Columbus dealt with this situation in the worst possible way, attempting to capture the Quibián and his family and chief men and carry them to Spain, believing that his subjects would then submit. A party of 70 to 80 men, led by the Adelantado and Méndez, rowed up the Río Veragua (x.12). In the foothills, where a slight gleam of white water shows in our air photograph, they surrounded the Quibián's village, captured him and about thirty of his household, and looted some 300 ducats' worth of gold objects. But the Quibián escaped when being taken downriver, his people aroused, and on 6 April, when three caravels had got out across the bar, about 400 Indians attacked Santa María de Belén. Their arrows and spears drove right through the wicker walls of the huts. Largely by aid of the Irish wolfhound, the attack was repulsed; but two boats from *Capitana*, led by her captain Diego Tristán, were ambushed upriver where the men were filling water casks, and all but one were slaughtered (x.13). Here was a tough situation. Three caravels were lying in the open roadstead outside the bar, at the mercy of any storm that might blow up; one (*Gallego*), which the Admiral intended to leave for the garrison's use, lay trapped inside. Indians continued to prowl about the settlement, raising horrid whoops and yells; and there were no hostages for their good behavior, since those imprisoned on board the flagship either escaped or hanged themselves in the hold. Columbus now realized that he had

made the Indians implacable enemies and that the trading post must be evacu-
ated or the garrison would meet the fate of Navidad. Having only one
small boat left, and that too deep to get over the bar, Columbus had to send
orders to his brother by a stout swimmer, Pedro de Ledesma.

X.13

The men ashore now abandoned Santa María de Belén, which was commanded from nearby heights, and built a stockade on a flat point at the entrance to the lagoon (x.14), arming it with two brass cannon to cover their retreat. These, and the wolfhound, kept the Indians at bay long enough for Diego Méndez to build a raft on which Bartholomew, all the men, the valuable dog and considerable stores were lightered across the bar and distributed among *Capitana, Santiago* and *Vizcaíno. Gallego* was abandoned, and the other three caravels sailed on 16 April 1503.

In subsequent years Felipe Gutiérrez and other conquistadors attempted in vain to subdue the natives of Veragua from the Pacific side. The crown in 1537 granted Veragua, between the Río Belén and Puerto Limón, to Don Luis Colón, the Admiral's worthless grandson, together with the title Duque de Veragua. In 1546, when Don Luis sent an expedition under Cristobal de Peña to secure his duchy, the Quibián's successor repelled it with heavy loss, and among those killed was Francisco Colón, another grandson of the Discoverer. Eleven years later, Don Luis leased his duchy to Francisco Vásquez de Coronado, who succeeded in establishing a settlement called Trinidad up the Río Belén; and another, La Concepción, at the mouth of one of the many rivers between the Veragua and the Chiriquí. Vásquez brought a coffle of slaves to extract the gold, and employed enough force to keep the natives at bay; but after his death in 1560 both settlements were abandoned. Every later

x.14

attempt to exploit the gold deposits has failed; surviving Veragua Indians have retired to the high mountains, and only miserable villages of Negroes at the river mouths mark the scenes of these high hopes and tragic events.

East of the Belén the fleet passed the mouth of the Coclé and at least fifteen other rivers flowing from the cordillera through heavy rain forest. On 17 December 1502 the fleet put in at a port which Columbus named Puerto Gordo. This was certainly Manzanillo Bay, harbor for the city of Colón, and for the United States naval base of Coco Solo; Ferdinand recorded, prophetically, that it was "like a *canale*" — a channel or canal (x.15). Here the fleet rested three days, then set sail, but was blown back by foul weather; and here it remained from Christmas Day 1502 to 8 January 1503. The Admiral well

x.16

named this Costa de los Contrastes, Coast of Contrarieties, uncertain weather, which it still is.[1] The 1865 *Sailing Directions for the Coast of Colombia,* to which Panama then belonged, warn the mariner, "Be constantly on your guard against the squalls" which "frequently shift from the land round the compass, with torrents of rain and gusts of wind, so as to oblige you to clew all up." So we found it in October 1963, and were very glad of our speed which enabled us to evade the squalls and nip into Tocumen Airfield, Panama.

[1] *Contrastes,* in nautical Spanish, means sudden changes of wind. We in Six-zero-Papa overshot Puerto Bello owing to a stormy tail wind, and had to backtrack.

Columbus was now very close to making a discovery which would have ranked in importance with his original one of 1492 — the Pacific Ocean. He noted the hundred-foot rocky headland at the mouth of the Río Chagres (x.16), named it El Peñon, and tried to anchor in the adjacent roadstead, but was blown out to sea. Had he ascended the Chagres by ship's boat and dugout, he could have reached a point only twelve or fifteen miles from the salt water of the Great South Sea. Why, then, did he not make the attempt? Partly because he was unable to communicate with the local Indians; they were shy tree dwellers, hard to get at, and nobody on board spoke their language; but mostly because the fleet had taken a terrible buffeting in December. The men, thoroughly exhausted — "lifeless," says Columbus — demanded surcease from work during Christmas week; and the Admiral, humbled by his failure to find The Strait, and suffering from arthritis, had no energy left. So, ignorant of how close he was to solving a major geographical secret, he departed from the future canal mouth, and Vasco Nuñez de Balboa won the glory of being the first European to cross the isthmus.

In the colonial era the Spanish government blasted off the top of El Peñon and built Fort Lorenzo there (x.17).

X.17

x.18

The next port eastward from the future canal that Columbus entered, and named, was Puerto Bello. That was immediately after his first visit to Veragua. Ferdinand says that he called it so "because it is very large and beautiful and well populated and surrounded by extensive cultivated country. He entered this place on 2 November, passing between two small islands [x.18]. Within ships may lay close aboard the shore and depart in a hurry if they wish." That is because the tradewind here blows offshore. "The country about the harbor and higher up is not very rough, but tilled and full of houses . . . and it looks like a painting, the prettiest that ever was seen." The people, though they had no gold, were friendly, exchanging provisions and skeins of spun cotton for pins and lace points. Ferdinand's description is not exaggerated, and Puerto Bello must indeed have looked good after the rugged shores of Veragua. The Spaniards later made it the northern terminus of their trans-isthmian mule track; and it is said that in the next century silver ingots from Peru were stacked like cordwood in the plaza. But today the surrounding country is sparsely cultivated (x.19). On his return passage from Belén, Columbus here abandoned *Vizcaíno* as hopelessly worm-eaten. Diego de Nicuesa found her carcass there six years later.

After spending seven days in this fine harbor, the fleet sailed around Punta Manzanillo and its two pretty *mogotes* (dumplings) (x.20) and put in at

another pretty, cultivated spot which Columbus named Puerto de Bastimentos, Harbor of Provisions (x.21). Nicuesa in 1508 renamed it Nombre de Dios, and that name has stuck. There they stayed almost two weeks; and, after a stop at the mouth of the Río Culebra to barter, put in at a port so closed in and secluded that the Admiral named it El Retrete. It is now Puerto Escribanos. One enters by a narrow channel, and inside the water is so deep that ships can lie against either shore (x.22). That feature almost proved the undoing of Columbus's sailors. In twos and threes, well armed, they stole away at night, marched to the villages, extorted gold and women, and provoked a native uprising. Columbus, after failing to appease a warlike assembly of vengeful Indians on the shore, was fain to disperse them by firing round shot into their midst.

These people, whom Ferdinand describes as the handsomest Indians they had yet encountered, were the Cuna Cuna, generally known as the San Blas nation. They have maintained their integrity to this day, dress much as Columbus described the Jicaque, adorn their womenfolk with gold disks, allow no white man to spend a night in one of their villages, and retain their language, their customs, their blood and their dignity. During the building of

X.21

the Panama Canal, a high official attempted to purchase the sand of one of the cays in this region, to use in construction. The reigning cacique replied, "He who made this sand made it for the Cuna Cuna who live no longer, for those who are here today and also for those to come. So it is not ours only, and we could not sell it."

The Panama government maintains a health center for the Cuna Cuna at Porvenir Island, where we show our *Capitana* at anchor (x.23), and the doctor with his young patients (x.24). They get about entirely by their home-made dugouts, much as their ancestors did, with the addition of sails and a

X.24

few "respectable" modifications which they picked up from the British — note the couple under a black umbrella in a dugout canoe, going to church; the men are wearing bowler hats (x.25, a,b). When Morison sailed along this coast in 1940 the latest thing in headgear was a boy's size bowler hat, an enterprising trader having bought quantities of them at a bargain, to exchange with the Indians for coconuts.

Near Puerto Escribanos, the fleet encountered the most severe tempest of this very rough voyage; whole gales, thunder and lightning, torrential rains, even a waterspout, which the Admiral exorcised by reading from his Bible the account of the tempest off Capernaum in John 6: 18-20. During ten or twelve days it was impossible to cook food on board, and the hardtack had become so wormy that, says Ferdinand, "God help me, I saw many men wait until nightfall to eat their porridge so as not to see the maggots in it."

[212]

x.25b

x.25a

Toward the end of April 1503, Columbus passed Retrete again in the two remaining caravels of his fleet, rounded Punta San Blas, and sailed outside the Archipelago de las Mulatas, the ragged line of wooded cays which the Admiral named Las Barbas, The Whiskers (x.26). Nobody who wrote about this voyage took time to record impressions of the magnificent scenery along this coast: the cordillera rising to three thousand feet straight from the sea, and clothed to the summit with glossy hardwoods — mahogany, cedar, silk-cotton, ebony, satinwood, rosewood and the brazil. Every so often one tree rises above the rolling sea of green foliage and bursts into a mass of brilliant blossoms, as though a torch were being held up from the dark jungle below.

One reason, doubtless, for this silence was a serious altercation between the Admiral and his officers. All were eager to make Hispaniola before the worm-eaten caravels sank under them; but how to get there? Columbus wished to sail along the coast eastward to some point already known, such as Margarita, whence he could be sure to fetch Hispaniola on the starboard tack. But the others, who had not kept a careful dead reckoning, insisted that they were already east of the Caribbees and must strike north at once or miss the islands and perish in the broad ocean.

For eight days they sailed along the Archipelago de las Mulatas; passing the site of Acla, Balboa's trading post whence he began his march across the isthmus, Golden Island, where Drake harbored in 1595, and Punta Escocés, site of the short-lived Scots colony of Darien (x.27). The coast now began to

X.27

trend southerly into the Gulf of Darien, and the people feared that the Admiral was taking them into some never-never land. After passing Punta de Mosquitos (x.28), they made such a row that when the two waterlogged caravels reached a promontory that the Admiral named El Mármol, The Marble

X.28

X.29

(x.29), he could resist their importunity no longer, and agreed to strike across the Caribbean for Hispaniola. So, after spending a Sunday night in the sheltered cove now called Zarzurro (x.30), south of the Cape and, doubtless, filling water casks from the little stream, "On Monday 1 May of this year 1503," states Ferdinand, "we stood to the northward, with winds and currents from the east."

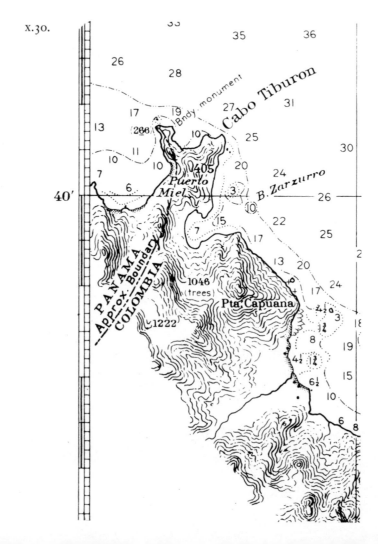

x.30.

We have no hesitation in positively identifying Columbus's last place of call on the mainland, El Mármol, as Cabo Tiburón, which now marks the boundary between the Republics of Colombia and Panama. It is true that every earlier writer has identified this spot as Punta de Mosquitos, Punta San Blas, or some other cape along the San Blas coast; but the reasons in favor of Cabo Tiburón are indisputable: (1) Ferdinand writes: "Thence, passing many others, to the end of the continent which we saw [and which] he called Marmoro, [and] which was some ten leagues beyond Las Barbas." [1] Cabo Tiburón does look like the end of a land mass as one approaches, whilst Punta de Mosquitos is merely one of many relatively inconspicuous promontories. (2) Cabo Tiburón, as our close-ups (x.31, 32) indicate, shows on its

[1] "Quindi passati più oltre al fine, che vedemmo di terra firma, chiamò Marmoro quello spatio che v'era di X leghe dalle Barbe." *Historie* (1571 ed.) ch. 100. El Mármol, of which Marmoro is the translation, appears on Peter Martyr's map of the New World of 1511. The distance of 10 leagues (31.8 nautical miles), too, is about right, presuming that Ferdinand meant the thickest part of the Archipelago de las Mulatas, which Columbus called Las Barbas.

x.31

cliffs conspicuous white patches and strata, which would have suggested *mármol* (marble) to Columbus; whilst Punta Mosquitos and all other capes within a hundred miles are completely muffled in verdure.

Before leaving this coast, Columbus must have seen some of the Indians whose descendants live today near the Colombia-Panama border. They are known as the Noaname or Southern Chocó nation. It will be observed that they use an odd sort of sharp-pointed paddle (x.33), and that they wear

X.33

silver ear-spools of the same style as the gold ones that Columbus observed on the "Coast of Ears" in Honduras (x.34). The girl is painted with the juice of a fruit called *jagua;* the beaded caps are traditional; and as Venetian glass beads were standard trading truck with Columbus, the Chocó very likely obtained their first beads from him.

x.34

Just as Cape Tiburón became the terminus of Columbus's mainland exploration, so for us in Six-zero-Papa it marked the end of a delightful tour along the coasts of Panama and Colombia. After photographing the cape, we flew to Bogotá in two hours; and our concluding photograph to this chapter (x.35) shows the four of us safely grounded at El Dorado airport, Bogotá.

x.35

CHAPTER XI

Jamaica[1]

OLUMBUS visited Jamaica thrice. He discovered it in 1494, as a diversion from his exploration of southern Cuba, returned in July to sail around it; and in 1503-04, on his Fourth Voyage, spent a year very unwillingly on the north coast.

The discovery took place on 5 May 1494, when, sailing south from Cape Cruz in *Niña* with *San Juan* and *Cardera*, the Admiral made out the entrance to St. Ann's Bay, between a barrier reef and what is now called Draxhall Point (xi.1). He named this place Santa Gloria, "on account of the extreme beauty of its glorious country, in comparison with which the gardens of

[1] Las Casas *Historia* ch. xciv says that Columbus named it Santiago; but that name did not stick. Ferdinand, Peter Martyr, Andrés Bernáldez and all other early authorities call it by the native name, spelling it Xaymaca, Xamaíca, and many other ways.

xi.1

Valencia are nothing." Thus Andrés Bernáldez transmits to us the Discoverer's enthusiasm over this island; and he continues: "It is the fairest island that eyes have beheld; mountainous and the land seems to touch the sky; very large, bigger than Sicily, has a circumference of 800 leagues (I mean miles) and all full of valleys and fields and plains; it is very strong and extraordinarily populous; even on the edge of the sea as well as inland it is full of very big villages very near together, about four leagues apart. They have more canoes than elsewhere in these parts, and the biggest that have yet been seen, all made each of a single tree trunk; and in all these parts every cacique has a great canoe for himself in which he takes pride as a Castilian gentleman is proud of possessing a fine, big ship. They have their canoes carved and painted both bow and stern with ornaments so that their beauty is marvellous; one of these big ones that the Admiral measured was 96 feet in length and 8 foot beam."

That canoe building is no lost art in Jamaica is shown by our air view over St. Ann's Bay (xi.2). Most of these boats are dugouts, and elsewhere in Jamaica the present natives, all Negroes, build the largest canoes in the Caribbean. With sand ballast and a homemade sail, a Jamaican canoe can make a speed as high as 15 knots on her way to the fishing grounds.

xi.2

Although the Jamaican Indians belonged to the same Arawak language group as those of Cuba and Hispaniola, and shared the same Taino culture, they were more warlike. When Columbus's caravels approached the mouth of St. Ann's Bay, sixty or seventy canoes full of shouting, gesticulating warriors paddled out to stop them. A blank cannon salvo sent the natives hastily paddling back into harbor. Columbus now sent Diego his Indian interpreter in a boat to try to appease them, which he accomplished so well that one canoe came aboard the flagship and received a handout of old clothes and trading truck.

Columbus then spent only one night at St. Ann's Bay; and we shall return thither shortly, as the Admiral did after eight years' absence. On 6 May he sailed 15 miles westward to a harbor "shaped like a horseshoe" which he named Puerto Bueno (xi.3) and which has the unique distinction among Jamaican ports of having kept its Columbian name. It is now Río Bueno Harbor. Here the Indians, wearing feather headdresses and palm-leaf corslets, made another hostile demonstration, hurling wooden spears at the caravels and throwing stones at the Spaniards as they touched land. Since the fleet needed wood and water, the Admiral decided to make the Indians "acquainted with the arms of Castile." This was easily effected by sending the ships' boats ashore with crossbowmen who "pricked them well and killed a number"; and when the Spaniards landed, they let loose a big dog "who bit them and did them great hurt, for a dog is worth ten men against Indians." Here is the first recorded instance of European tactics with Indians that became common; and on Columbus's later voyages big mastiffs or wolfhounds were always shipped for this particular purpose.

Next day, six Indians came down to the shore with propitiatory gifts of cassava, fruit and fish, which the Admiral graciously accepted. During the rest of their stay at Río Bueno the Spaniards were well furnished with provisions, and the Indians with trading truck. Here, as elsewhere in Jamaica, the Admiral was disappointed at finding no gold ornaments among the natives' apparel nor (until he met the cacique at Portland Bight) any trace of the precious metal.

On 9 May 1494 the fleet sailed westward to Montego Bay, which the Admiral named El Golfo de Buen Tiempo, Fair Weather Gulf (xi.4). This name proved to be prophetic, Montego Bay having become the leading Jamaican winter resort; but it must have seemed singularly unpropitious at that time. An unseasonable, rainy westerly wind made up; so Juan de la Cosa, who was on board *Niña*, names Montego "Malabahía," or Bad Bay, on his world map. This turn of foul weather determined Columbus to postpone further exploration of Jamaica, and to return to Cuba, as we have described in Chapter IV.

xi.4

On 21 July the same three caravels again took off from Cape Cruz, to explore Jamaica. They made Montego Bay without difficulty. Thence they sailed west, past little Lucea harbor (xi.5), around Negril Point, the western promontory of the island (xi.6), and then along the south coast, past the

xi.7

modern Savanna-la-Mar, Black River, Pedro Bluff (xi.7), and the mouth of
the Minho River (xi.8). Columbus spent nineteen days in this reconnaissance,
anchoring every night because the caravels were struggling against the pre-
vailing wind. They could make progress only by leaving an anchorage before dawn with the land breeze, beating eastward as best they could, and
nipping into harbor when the tradewind made up strong. The Admiral more
than once adverted to the difficulty of sailing eastward in the Caribbean,
where both wind and currents run westerly. And that trouble existed
throughout the days of sail. William Hickey, living on the south shore of

xi.8

Jamaica toward the end of the eighteenth century, tells of watching a ship trying to make easting. Every day she stood out to sea close-hauled on the port tack, and every evening she returned on the starboard tack to the same position. This went on for eight days without gaining a mile.

Contemporary accounts afford us no details of Columbus's struggle along the south shore of Jamaica until, on or about 18 August, he made Portland Bight (xi.9), which for no apparent reason (since there were no cows in Jamaica) he named Bahía de la Vaca. This bay runs ten miles up into the land. The Admiral recorded that it contained seven islets; and there are, indeed, seven big ones, some with salt ponds, and several small ones; and he observed that the shore was lined with Indian villages. He probably anchored

xi.9

in the inner Galleon Harbor, behind Goat Island (xi.10). The curious verdure in the foreground is mangrove, and illustrates how that useless shrub spreads over sand or mud flats when protected from waves.

The natives were most friendly; here occurred the picturesque and pathetic incident which Bernáldez describes. Three canoes came aboard the caravels just as they were weighing to depart. In the largest canoe, beautifully decorated with carvings, was a cacique with his wife, two sons, five brothers — and two very beautiful daughters, completely naked — as the wife was except "for a little cotton thing no bigger than an orange peel." A tall Indian, as herald, stood erect at the bow, wearing a cloak of red feathers and a feather coronet and holding a white banner. The rest of the crew were appareled in feather garments, and the cacique wore a big ornament of guanín, which he must have obtained by trade from the mainland.

xi.10

When the canoes drew alongside, Columbus was in his cabin, and did not emerge until the Indians were on board. As soon as the cacique saw the Admiral, he declared that he and his family wished to sail home with him and visit the Sovereigns, "and to see the wonders of Castile" so eloquently described by Diego the interpreter. He had even sent his canoes ashore, expecting, with his suite, to be accepted as passengers. The cacique brought no traveling gear, innocently assuming that the voyage to Spain would be short and the weather like that of Jamaica. Columbus, to his credit, resisted the temptation to parade this royal family of Jamaica before his Sovereigns. He doubtless thought of what the wife and daughters might expect from rough seamen, and of the disillusion awaiting these poor souls in Spain, if indeed they survived the cold weather and hardships of the transatlantic voyage. So he sent them ashore in the caravel's barge, after receiving their homage and fealty to Ferdinand and Isabella.

Portland Bight eventually became the principal harbor for Spanish Jamaica; but on proceeding easterly Columbus missed Port Royal Bay, the harbor of Kingston, which became an English metropolis and is now the capital of independent Jamaica. He passed Port Morant and the site of the grass strip where Six-zero-Papa made an emergency landing (xi.11) and her

crew took refuge in a hut from a tropical rainstorm (xi.12). Since the Blue
Mountains were concealed by a cloud cover, as often happens in August,
Columbus was not aware that he was close to the highest mountain in the
West Indies. Morant Point, the eastern cape of Jamaica, he named El Cabo
del Farol, the Cape of the Light, probably because the Indians lighted a

xi.12

watchfire there. Our photograph, taken just around this point, shows a hill
which local historians believe to have been the headquarters of the cacique
Huareno, from whom Diego Méndez obtained the big canoes for crossing
to Hispaniola (xi.13).

Some 32 miles south by east from that point lie the low Morant Cays.
Columbus's four caravels on his Fourth Voyage were carried thither by the
current in a calm, on 17 July 1502. The men rowed ashore to look for
fresh water, seldom to be found in low, sandy cays; but holes dug by the
sailors filled up with sweet water, for which reason Columbus named these

xi.13

cays Las Islas de los Pozos, Isles of the Wells (xi.14). The British *Sailing Directions for the West Indies*, published almost four centuries later, advises seamen to do just as the Spaniards did, if they want fresh water.

Let us now return to the north coast of Jamaica where, as to "any port in a storm," Columbus was glad to arrive in 1503; and where, contrary to intention, he spent an entire year.

After his failure to establish a colony in Veragua (see Chapter IX), the Admiral, abandoning his two most unseaworthy and waterlogged caravels,

xi.14 attempted to cross the Caribbean to Hispaniola. The winds and currents carried him west of his destination, and on 10 May he passed between the Cayman Islands (xi.15), which Ferdinand described as "very small and low," with the sea so full of turtles that their backs "looked like little rocks." And the turtle fishery is a leading industry in the Caymans today (xi.16). After spending a blowy night in the harbor between Cays Bretón and Cinco Balas off Cuba and beating painfully eastward, the two caravels took off for Jamaica from a harbor near Cape Cruz. Teredos had worked on the bottoms of *Capitana* and

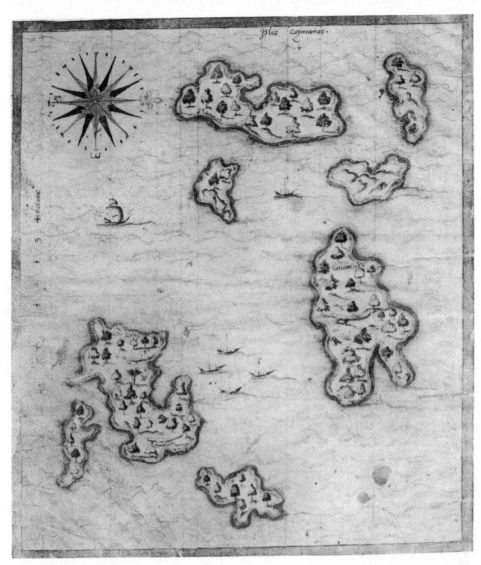

Santiago with such success that they were kept from sinking only (as an old shipmate said of a rotten yacht) "by the teredos holding hands." As the Admiral's son, who was with him, recorded, "Day and night we never ceased working three pumps in each of them, and if any broke down, we had to supply its place by bailing with kettles." On the night of 22 June the water was almost up to *Capitana's* deck, but in the morning they made a port on the north coast of Jamaica that was well named by the English, Dry Harbor (xi.17), but in the interest of the tourist trade has lately been renamed Discovery Bay.

A dry harbor it was, no fresh water to be had; so the Spaniards, after laboriously bailing out their vessels again, took advantage of a fortunate westerly to run along the coast to Santa Gloria (St. Ann's Bay), where Columbus had first anchored in Jamaican waters nine years before.

He remembered that this place had fresh water; and as the waterlogged caravels wallowed along, in momentary danger of foundering, the Admiral observed that behind the barrier reef was a shelving beach, and behind that smoke rose, indicating an Indian village. So, after entering the main harbor, where the present town of St. Ann's is located, he rowed or kedged the

caravels to this spot inside the barrier reef. Here *Capitana* and *Santiago* were run ashore, their stone ballast thrown out and their hulls hauled high and dry by attaching cables to trees and working the windlass. The men then unbent their sails and covered the decks with them, helped out by palm-leaf shelters as protection from the weather. Thus the two caravels were transformed into grounded houseboats. This beach was shielded from ocean surges by the barrier reef, yet had a spacious outlook so that any passing sail could be hailed — but none appeared until the following year. Columbus had accurately reported that neither gold nor pearls were to be had in Jamaica, so the Spaniards now swarming into the New World to reap the fruits of his discoveries were not interested in this island.

Our photograph (xi.18) of the beach whence these caravels never budged shows, in the background, a plantation named New Seville; it was here that Spanish colonists built their first Jamaican town, Nueva Sevilla, in 1508. Its ruins are still there, concealed by a coconut plantation; and a statue of the Discoverer has been erected by the Catholic Bishop of Jamaica at a crossroad near the clearing.

Another advantage for the Spaniards was the presence nearby of an Indian village called Maima, whose natives were friendly and, for a time, coöperative; they furnished the 120 Christians with cassava bread, maize, fish, and the little rodent called hutía, in exchange for the usual trading truck of hawk's bells, beads, red caps, cheap mirrors and scissors. Apparently the Spaniards were too lazy or incompetent to fish or plant for themselves, and they insisted on enormous quantities of food, according to native standards. Ferdinand said that a Spaniard would eat more in one day than an Indian could in a week. So Indian consumer demand was more than satisfied in seven months, and the customers stopped bringing food to the beached caravels. Columbus, faced with possible famine, persuaded them to resume trade by using his head and his almanac. Predicting to an Indian delegation a total eclipse of the moon

xi.18

on the night of 29 February 1504, as a sign of God's wrath for withholding provisions from His chosen people, he readily obtained their promise to resume food deliveries as his price for interceding with the Almighty to restore the moon's light.

In the meantime two of the Admiral's captains, Diego Méndez of Segura and Bartolomeo Fieschi of Genoa, had volunteered to seek help from Hispaniola in native canoes, with Indian paddlers. A ship's boat would have been more seaworthy, but Columbus had lost all his boats. Two big dugouts were selected, provided with false keels to increase stability, washboards to keep out the spray, and even sails. After one false start, Méndez and Fieschi, with several Indians in each canoe, took off from St. Ann's about the end of July, 1503. Several other canoes, commanded by Bartholomew Columbus, escorted them along the north coast, since most of the natives between St. Ann's and Morant Point were unfriendly. They passed some of the finest scenery in Jamaica: waterfalls emptying directly into the sea (xi.19), fertile valleys,

xi.19

rugged cliffs on which the surges broke and roared (xi.20), little harbors where they could get rest for a night after struggling against wind and sea all day (xi.21). After paddling a good hundred miles, they reached the point that they judged to be nearest to Hispaniola, said farewell to Bartholomew and their escort *con muchas lagrimas* — with abundant tears — and hopefully took their departure.

This crossing of the Windward Passage at its widest part was tough for all hands. On the second night out, an Indian who had consumed all his water rations died of thirst, and others jumped overboard. But when the moon rose on the third evening, Méndez observed that its lower limb was covered by a

xi.21

little island, as in an eclipse. That island was Navassa (xi.22). This encouraged the survivors to keep on, and on the morning of the fourth day they managed to land on Navassa, climb the rocks, find fresh water in the hollows, and light a fire with flint and steel to cook shellfish. One may say that this little barren island saved the lives of Columbus and his men; for no Christian knew what had happened to their fleet since it left Hispaniola in July 1502. Thus, had the canoes not got through, all hands in Jamaica would have been left there indefinitely.

From Navassa the mountains of Hispaniola were visible, so on the evening of the same day the canoes were launched again, and the remaining thirty miles to Cape Tiburón were covered before morning. But Don Nicolás de Ovando, Viceroy of Hispaniola, wishing to ensure that Columbus never return to the island that he discovered, threw sundry difficulties in the way of Méndez's obtaining a caravel to rescue the Admiral, and ten more months elapsed before he obtained one.

xi.22

In the meantime, a mutiny led by the brothers Porras had broken out in Jamaica among Columbus's men, who fancied that they were being detained unnecessarily. After wandering about the island, abusing the Indians and trying in vain to make the canoe trip to Hispaniola on their own, the rebels attacked the Columbus brothers and their loyal men hard by the beached caravels. Indians from the village of Maima swarmed around the field of battle to enjoy the spectacle of Christians slashing and stabbing each other with swords, daggers and knives, since their gunpowder had long since been expended. The loyalists won, and Columbus pardoned the rebels. Casualties were not great, only four men killed or died of wounds; but one of these was Captain Pedro de Terreros, the Admiral's most loyal and able captain, who had been with him on all four voyages. Pedro de Ledesma, one of the leading mutineers, had "a wound in his head through which one could see his brains . . . and one foot was sliced from heel to toe like the sole of a slipper." Yet he recovered, and some years later piloted the younger Pinzón on a voyage to Honduras.

De Bry's engraving of this battle (xi.23), which appeared in his *Collectiones Peregrinationum* of 1540, we reproduce only to show how wrong in almost every detail these early illustrators were. Even the Indians, in square-cut canoes, look like Dutchmen!

Almost one year to a day after Columbus arrived at St. Ann's Bay, there appeared a *caravelón* chartered by Méndez for rescue. Christopher, Bartholomew, Ferdinand and the 107 other survivors, both loyal men and mutineers, managed to find room on board this tiny vessel. On 29 June she sailed from Santa Gloria for Santo Domingo, and that passage consumed six and a half weeks. Columbus chartered another caravel at Santo Domingo, and with as many survivors as chose to accompany him (a number had had enough and stayed in Hispaniola), suffered a tough 56-day homeward passage, reaching Sanlúcar near the mouth of Seville river on 7 November 1504.

From Sanlúcar the Admiral, feeling very spent and ill, proceeded to his favorite hospice, the monastery of Las Cuevas at Seville. He had not long been there when he received bad news, the death of his patroness Queen Isabella. During the remaining eighteen months of Columbus's life, while his arthritis grew worse, his main endeavor was to have his titles and privileges

Insula Iamaica

Franciscus Poraz

Christophorus Columbus

xi.23

restored. His dream was to have Ovando sent packing, and himself, the right-ful Viceroy of the Indies and Admiral of the Ocean Sea, return in triumph to Santo Domingo and die in the city that he and his brother had founded. To that end, in the spring of 1505, as soon as he was well enough to travel by muleback, he followed Ferdinand's court from place to place. All was in vain. The King did eventually send the Discoverer's son Don Diego, who had married one of his cousins, to Santo Domingo; but he would do nothing for the man who for Spain had discovered a New World.

Finally, on 20 May 1506, in an obscure house at Valladolid, in the presence of his sons and his loyal captains Méndez and Fieschi, the Discoverer of the New World received the viaticum, muttered *In manus tuas, Domine, commendo spiritum meum*, and gave up the ghost.

We have but meager details on those pitiful last months of Columbus's life. One imagines that, asleep or unconscious, the Admiral fancied himself on the quarterdeck of his flagship, giving orders for the master to pass on to the crew. Knowing his appreciation of natural beauty, one may be certain that he lived again his fair-weather sails in that Terrestrial Paradise, the Caribbean — cloud masses on the mountains, rainbows bridging the valleys, peacock-like colors of the sea, sand beaches gleaming in the sun, sparkling rivers and gushing waterfalls, hardwood trees thrusting their blossoms above green foliage. Most of all he would have remembered the triumph of the first landfall, when he shared with his men the greatest discovery yet made in human history; and those gorgeous winter days of the Second Voyage, so full of hope before the tragedy of Navidad became known, when in his gallant fleet he gaily sailed from one superb island to another. As he lay sleepless on his bed of pain, a star glimpsed through the window might recall to Columbus the calm, warm tropic nights when his caravels lay quietly at anchor in the lee of the land, stars of incredible brightness shone overhead, and hearty voices joined in the hymn *Salve Regina* to the Queen of Heaven.

Index

ABBREVIATIONS

B. Bahía, Baie, Bay
C. Cabo, Cap, Cape
C.C. Christopher Columbus
D. Don, Doña
Fr. Father, Fray
G. Golfo, Gulf
I., Is. Ile(s), Isla(s), Island(s), Isle(s)

Mt. Monte, Mountain
Pen. Peninsula
Pt., Pta., Pte. Point, Punta, Pointe
Pto. Port, Puerto
R. Río, River
U. University
V. Voyage